Cape Coast "Abɔɔdzen Kurow Mu"

The Town of Romanticised Finesse

(Reminiscences of the mid 30's and 40's)

by

Mrs Augustina Korsah

This is a work of fiction based on substantive historical and personal real life events, surrounded by the geographical background of Cape Coast town. The characters, incidents and dialogue are largely products of the author's imagination however certain scenes and settings actually existed in and around Cape Coast, therefore as this work contains personal experiences, any resemblance to events or persons living is inevitable and may be entirely coincidental.

www.trafford.com

North America & international
toll-free: 844-688-6899 (USA & Canada)
fax: 812 355 4082

TABLE OF CONTENTS

CHAPTER III

POST WAR YEARS: 1939–1945

CHAPTER IV

COLONIAL PRE-INDEPENDENCE ERA/SOCIAL & CULTURAL ASPECTS

DEDICATION

This book is dedicated to:

my son and mentor Mr Kwesi Kyir Korsah a.k.a. "Yokwesi".
and to my daughters
Ms Ione Korsah, Ms Valerie Korsah and Mrs Lynda Osafo (neé Korsah)
who have given me their support in various ways,
throughout the writing of this book.
I pray that the Lord Almighty blesses all of them
with the Fruit of the Holy Spirit

PURPOSE OF THIS WORK

This book was penned in order that we make an attempt at conserving our cultural heritage through any means of communication possible, and also in order that:

- the Youth of today should be encouraged to aim high to achieve a sound education and reap the benefits thereof;

- the Youth should show respect for elders at all times, be well disciplined and acquire good morals in order to avoid:
  - AIDS – Acquired Immune Deficiency Syndrome;
  - HIV – Human Immuno Deficiency Virus;
  - STDs – Sexually Transmitted Diseases e.g. Gonorrhoea, Syphilis;

- African-American tourists and other interested parties world-wide should endeavour to one day discover the treasure that is **Cape Coast a.k.a. "Abɔɔdzen Kurow Mu: The Town of Romanticised Finesse** in order to enrich their knowledge of the nature, culture and traditions of the people of Ghana (formerly the British colony of The Gold Coast).

AUTHOR'S HISTORY

Mrs Augustina Angela Lilian Korsah (neé Buckle) was born and raised in Cape Coast where she attended Government Girls' School and completed her elementary education with distinction. She was awarded a scholarship to Achimota College (now Achimota Secondary School) where she obtained the Cambridge School Certificate.

After completing a post-secondary teacher training course at Achimota Training College, Mrs Korsah was posted to Kumasi[1] Government Girls' School. She also taught at various reputable international primary schools in Accra, namely Ridge Church School, Christ The King School and Faith Montessori School. For a number of years, Mrs Korsah also taught pupils at the Marina International School in Banjul, The Gambia, where she participated fully in meaningful workshops (which were based on the British National Curriculum), organised by expatriate female members of staff. She has over twenty years teaching experience to her credit, and is now a retired Educationist resident in Accra[2], Ghana.

---

[1]   Kumasi is the capital town of the Ashanti Region (also known as the Garden City).

[2]   Accra is the capital city of Ghana, West Africa

FOREWORD: By children of the Author

We, the daughters and son of Mrs Augustina Korsah, soon became aware of the knowledge, expertise and dedication which was part and parcel of the package we knew as our Mother. Throughout her life and work she loved to educate and impart knowledge to any children she happened to meet in her chosen profession as an Educationist. Her well-known methodologies were best placed to bring out the best in her pupils, and particularly because she wanted her children to benefit from said expertise, we invariably found ourselves in her class at some point during our primary school education!

Mrs Korsah is a disciplinarian and her classes helped prepare pupils for the basics needed to pass the dreaded Common Entrance Examination (an examination necessary to enter into any secondary school in Ghana, West Africa). Her pupils remember Mrs Korsah for her dedication and drive in obtaining the best out of her pupils and because of her methods of teaching, she has instilled in them the confidence to offer their best wherever they live in the world, to this day.

This book was inspired from discussions between mother and son (in London circa 1998) when her only son, Yokwesi, asked his mother about her teenage life in Cape Coast. Typical of Mother, she corrected him by stating "In those days they were not teenagers but 'young adolescents' or Nkataasia (for girls) and Mbɛrɛntsɛɛ (for boys). Discussions then continued about the "good old days" and gradually the idea of a novel based on Mother's reminiscences was formed.

"*Cape Coast a.k.a. Abɔɔdzen Kurow Mu: The Town of Romanticised Finesse*" is a great attempt to encapsulate the very essence and nature of the Fantse people and the intention is that this 'picture' travels across the pages of this book. We therefore hope you will enjoy and appreciate reading about scenes imaginary or otherwise based on true situations and facts in and around Cape Coast during the youth and lifetime of our mother as well as the many distinguished personalities mentioned herein.

PERSONAL ACKNOWLEDGEMENTS

The writing of this book required considerable research. My very special thanks to those who have been so wonderfully helpful.

My grateful thanks to:

1. Mrs Wilhelmina Bentsi-Enchill, a gracious lady for her priceless experiences, knowledge (about births), customary marriage and funeral rites in Cape Coast.

2. Professor Dorothy Jane Ffoulkes-Crabbe, only daughter of Mrs Mercy Kwarley Ffoulkes-Crabbe of blessed memory, who was Headmistress of Government Girls' School ("G.G.S"), Cape Coast, for twenty-seven years. "Nana" as we affectionately call her, has an abiding love for Cape Coast where she lived and had her primary education. She has sweet memories of a blissful enjoyable childhood especially as a 'Brownie' in the Girl Guides. I thank her for her contribution.

3. Mrs Emelia Atterh, twin daughter of Cape Coast parents, who lived among the native fisher-folk near the Cape Coast castle and I thank Mrs Atterh for her explicit and fascinating insight into their lifestyle. She also attended the first Catholic day and boarding school for girls in Cape Coast.

4. Mrs Doris Anin (neé Dadzie) affectionately called "Nana Foriwa" for brief profile of her late father Kofi Mensah Dadzie Esq., and for his photograph. Doris Anin had both her elementary and secondary education at Wesley Girls High School, Capecoast. She also travelled abroad for further studies and is now a retired West African Liaison Officer. She also is a member of the Royal Commonwealth Society for the Blind and a Director of the Ghana Society for the Blind.

5. Mrs Esi Arthur (neé Annan) (Sister of Kofi Annan), for her younger brother's youthful Photograph No. 10. - A proud son of Cape Coast who has risen to become the **United Nations Secretary General, Kofi Annan**. Esi Arthur had her elementary education at Wesley Girls High School Cape Coast. Her secondary education was, amongst others, at St. Monica Secondary School, Ashanti Mampong.

6. Dr (Mrs) Mary Stoove Grant (neé Duncan) for her brief profile and photograph. Mary Grant had her elementary education at Elmina and Obuasi Methodist Schools. Her secondary education was at Wesley Girls High School Cape Coast, and other institutions of education both at home and abroad. She qualified as a Fantse female medical doctor - a great achievement in those days. Dr Mary Grant rose to become a Member of the Council of State.

7. Professor J.O.M. Pobee and Dr (Mrs) Lucy M. Pobee, for the brief profile and photograph of the Professor's late father Mr John Mends Samuel Pobee – a distinguished brilliant educationist and scholar. Dr Joseph Orleans Mends Pobee popularly referred to as "Uncle Joe" was Professor of Medicine and Therapeutics of the University of Ghana Medical School and WHO[3] Consultant on Education assigned to the University of Zambia.

8. Supi Ebow Bentsi-Enchill (Lawyer), for the youthful photograph of his elder sister, the late Mrs Elizabeth Frances Sey (neé Biney). Mrs Sey was the first Fantse female graduate of the University College of the Gold Coast. She had her elementary education at St. Monica's School, Cape Coast and her secondary education was at Achimota College where she later taught for many years.

9. Mrs Ama Yawson (neé Bentsi-Enchill) affectionately called "Mymaa" for photographs of her late father, Kofi Bentsi-Enchill Esq, and his "Adaaso" residence.
    Brief Profile: Mymaa had her elementary education at Wesley Girls High School, Primary section Cape Coast. Her secondary education was at Holy Child Secondary School, Cape Coast where she travelled abroad for further studies.

10. Mrs Alberta Quartey (neé Nicholas) for her brief profile of her late father Reverend Canon Nicholas and for supplying a photograph of Reverend Nicholas.
    Brief Profile: Alberta Quartey had her elementary education at St. Monica's School, Cape Coast. Her secondary education was at St. Monica Secondary School, Ashanti Mampong. She attended other institutions both at home and abroad. She is presently the proprietress of Alsyd Academy – a primary school of high repute. My special thanks to her for graciously accepting to review the book: Cape Coast **Abɔɔdzen Kurow Mu**: The Town of Romanticised Finesse: Reminiscences of the mid 30's and 40's.

11. Mrs Heather Badger, who designed my original Book cover.

12. Adolph H. Agbo , *"Values of Adinkra Symbols"*, *1999;* Ebony Designs and Publications; pp1–3.

13. Ghana Tourist Board – Supply of Map of Ghana.

––

CHAPTER I
THE CULTURE AND TRADITIONS OF THE PEOPLE OF CAPE COAST

1. **EXPLANATION OF THE BOOK COVER DESIGN**

Sankofa: The Symbol of positive reversion and revival

Adinkra Symbols: Symbols are multi-functional in nature and are appreciated for both their aesthetic and communicative values. The Adinkra symbols are a large collection of mostly non-verbal illustrations of proverbs, parables and maxims which portray the educational, historical, moral values and philosophical thinking and way of life of Ghanaians. The Adinkra symbols have been used particularly by the Asantes for many years and date back many generations. The indigenous and well-known Adinkra cloth-producing villages are situated at Asokwa and Ntonso in the Ashanti Region, near Kumasi (capital city of Ashanti). The word "Adinkra" means 'farewell' or 'good-bye' in the Akan language, however Adinkra designs are presently used to celebrate births, christenings, weddings and all other important occasions in contemporary life within Ghana.

The **Sankɔfa** symbol is one of the many adinkra symbols used by the Ghanaian population and literally translates from the Akan[4] language to mean 'Go back and take'. *'Sankɔ'* - go back, *'Fa'* - take. The Sankɔfa symbol teaches the wisdom of learning from the right use of the positive contributions of the past in order to help build a better future. It also teaches people to cherish and value their culture and avoid its adulteration. The Sankɔfa symbol is the symbol of positive reversion and revival.

The golden colour of the book cover denotes the richness of memories recorded in *"Cape Coast "Abɔɔdzen Kurow Mu: The Town of Romanticised Finesse"*. While depicting the priceless collection of reminiscences from days gone by, this book also includes information about the inherent culture of the Fantse people.

The Sankɔfa symbol first appears in the sky quietly hovering above the sprawling hills and plains of Cape Coast town and its adjoining villages which are basking in the sunshine that gently caresses the coastal town. The significance of the theme of connecting the present with useful past values, is further reinforced by the reflection of the Sankɔfa symbol in water - a kind of "double billing". The pictorial representation of the sea and coastline is used as a background because this is synonymous with Cape Coast being a city situated on the coast.

---

[4]   Akan is a blanket term used to describe the vernacular language spoken by the tribes who live in the Ashanti, Central, Western and Eastern regional areas of Ghana.

2.   **APPELLATION OF THE PEOPLE OF CAPE COAST**

<u>Fantse Version</u>
OGUAA AKɔTɔ

"Oguaa Akɔtɔ dwerdwerba a wɔda hɔn tu ano. Apem nye eduasa koe a, apem enntum eduasa. Eyɛɛ Oguaa dɛn na Oguaa annyɛ wo bi?

<u>English translation</u>
The Oguaa People

The Spirit of the Oguaa people
Symbolised by the Indomitable Crab
A thousand waged war against thirty, and the thirty triumphed
What would you do to Oguaa that Oguaa would not fight back?"

A GENEROUS and KIND PEOPLE: For most inhabitants of Cape Coast, the best from foreigners was humbly reciprocated in diverse subtle ways by the indigenous people. Everywhere, people were treated courteously, especially the strangers who lived amongst them. For example, for months at a time, several day secondary students who came from other towns in the country would hire rooms (at very reasonably rents) in many neighbourhoods. By so doing, the students were able to avoid paying boarding school fees, which expense was considerably higher than the hiring of rooms. Two or four students might rent one room in a house and share the kitchen and bathroom with other members of the family who lived in the same house. The housewife provided free meals to the students each day when they had completed the long walk back from school, tired and hungry. The meagre rent of about six shillings a month went a long way in helping the host family with their household bills and the arrangement was also of benefit to the day students.

THE CULTURE AND TRADITIONS OF THE PEOPLE OF CAPE COAST

3.   INTRODUCTION TO CAPE COAST

CAPE COAST (a town in the Central Region), dubbed "Abɔɔdzen Kurow Mu" by its inhabitants, was the capital of the Gold Coast before the capital city was transferred to Accra in the Greater Accra Region. Cape Coast was spoken of as such because of its rich Fantse language and the genteel lifestyle of its people. It is remarkable that even the illiterates spoke and acted graciously. Cape Coast was also know as *"Cabo Corso"* by the Portuguese and its literal meaning was 'short cape'. This title was later corrupted and became known as 'Cape Coast'. The inhabitants of Cape Coast rightfully called it *"Oguaa"* which means a 'market place'. In modern day terms, "Oguaa" is the generic term referred to by the Fanste people when referring, in vernacular, to the town of Cape Coast.

e.g.   **Fantse language**:   "Merekɔ Oguaa anapa"
        English language   "I am going to Cape Coast in the morning".

From the many wooded hills in and around Cape Coast such as Ebenezer Hill, McCarthy Hill and Prospect Hill, to mention a few, one could see the Atlantic Ocean. On its beach stood the imposing Cape Coast Castle of slave trade fame which still stands to this day. The Castle served as the main Post Office and Prison for the whole town.

Road Names: Cape Coast had some fascinating names for their streets and roads. Here are a few of them:

Coronation Street
Commercial Street
Green Lattice Lane
Jackson Street
Jerusalem Street
Kawanopaado Place (Literal translation "*Close your mouth*" place) – a popular meeting venue.
Kotokuraba Road
London Bridge
Royal Lane
Tantri Road.

4.   CAPE COAST FOLK

In several of the villages in the hinterland lived most of the farming folk. The villagers would walk several miles, starting at dawn, from their villages to the main town carrying their farm produce on their heads for sale in **Kotokuraba Market** and **Anaafo Market** – the two main markets in Cape Coast. Failing this, villagers would go from house to house peddling their wares. The currency used in the English colony of The Gold Coast was Sterling pounds, shillings and pence[5].

The most important food item sold in Cape Coast markets was known as 'Fantse kenkey' of which a special type named "Akrɔnkɔ" was very popular because of its distinctive taste and aroma which endeared it to the Fantse people.

Some of the nearby villages were Siwudu, Adisadel, Pedu, Abura, Eyifua, Kakomdo, Mpɛasɛm, Yaayaakwano and Brafo Yaw. Others were Yamoransa, Amosima, Nkamfoa and Eguaase.

5.   THE FISHER FOLK OF CAPE COAST

Along the coast were the fishing villages of Moree, Queen Anne's Point and Iture, to mention a few. Ntsin, "Bentsir" and "Nkum" were communities who lived near the sea, and not too far away from the Castle and they were basically fisher folk.

The men folk paddled their wooden canoes to go fishing and on their return, the nets were dragged to the shore. Their women folk took over, collected the fish and placed them in woven baskets. As there was a lack of any form of cold storage facility available on the beach, the fresh fish was immediately sold to waiting vendors while the unsold fish was then either smoked, fried or cured with salt and dried in the sun (a chore performed by the women) to be sold in the market later on that day. Often the fishermen refused to sell delicious species of fish to customers, instead keeping it for themselves to eat at home. The Fantse language spoken by these fishermen and their women was of a special dialect, the vocabulary peculiar to them only.

As a general rule in Ghana, fishermen do not go fishing on Tuesday as it was considered a taboo to do so, and a sign of respect to their numerous gods and goddesses. Instead, on Tuesdays, the men rested and mended their nets while their sons played games of tug-of-war or wrestling on the beach.

---

[5]   Twelve pence made a shilling and twenty shillings made a pound.

On a working week day as soon as the men returned from sea; tired and hungry, their wives would hurriedly prepare a special plain soup called "*Apofo Anto*," with onion, pepper and salt only, as main ingredients, with very tasty fresh fish added to the soup, and in no time at all, it was ready to be eaten with kenkey, as "fufu" pounding took too long.

An alternative fresh fish stew using onions, pepper, tomatoes, salt and palm oil, was soon ready and eaten with kenkey. This fresh fish stew dish (made using palm oil) became known as "*Fantse-Fantse*".

These fisher folk had their own peculiar lifestyles and indulged in more traditional activities. Majority of them were idol worshippers and very few allowed themselves to be converted to Christianity.

The fisher folk were not particularly well-to-do and a family of parents, siblings and others, lived in small units of one bedroom in a compound house[6]. An idol they worshipped within the animist cult, would be located in a corner of the room screened off with dark cloth to protect from prying eyes. Each year fetish priests would oversee the pouring of libation and the killing of a fowl whereupon the fowl's blood would be smeared on the 'bosom' of the idol. A specially prepared dish known as "כהכ" (which was boiled and mashed yam mixed with palm oil) was prepared and eaten with boiled eggs. These acts were done to appease the gods who were called on for the protection of the fishermen as they went fishing on the high seas in their wooden canoes.

Most of the indigenous farmers and fisher folk were illiterate, but they were a joyous, hardworking people who fed the population well and were contented with their lot.

6.   ASAFO COMPANIES:

The seven main "Asafo Companies" or "Native Warriors" (as they were otherwise known) had their own flags, colourful uniforms and symbols. "Safohen" or "Supi" were leaders of these warriors. A specially trained flag-bearer would dance the intricate steps with the flag, which was not allowed to touch the ground and specialists groups would sing Asafo songs of various unique Fantse dialects which were full of innuendoes and insinuations.

Communication was by drumming for the announcement of war, a fire outbreak, death by drowning etc. and each message with its particular rhythm and beat was promptly responded to by the villagers.

---

[6]   A compound house is a walled building with several individual rooms/units leading out into a shared courtyard.

The three most popular Asafo companies were Ntsin, Bentsir and Nkum. The outdooring ceremonies of a newly installed "Safohen" was a colourful spectacle. On this occasion, the chief sat in a palanquin richly attired and carried high on the shoulders of specially appointed persons through the town, amidst dancing, drumming and singing in the streets of several neighbourhoods. The ceremony was followed later with feasting and merrymaking well into the night. Cape Coast hospitality was at its best. A bevy of beautiful young women, fashionably dressed, would be in attendance at the feast, smiling, chatting and serving all guests including gate-crashers.

===

7. THE FANTSE LANGUAGE SPOKEN IN CAPE COAST

The Fantse Language spoken in Cape Coast was a dialect with gentle pronunciations, soft syllables and intonations which were romantic and pleasing to the ear and included a sprinkling of English words. Here would be an example of a conversation between two young adolescent boys we shall name, Ato and Fiifi:

English translation:
Ato: "*I met a certain girl yesterday Fiifi, who was very good-looking. So I addressed her thus: "Sister girl, you are breathtakingly beautiful". "Thank you", she replied, with a smile and then elegantly shimmied away*".
Fiifi: "*So did she dazzle you with her dainty footsteps?*"
Ato: "*I dare say, they were wonderful to behold!*"

Fante version example:
Ato: "Mehyiaa 'some girl' bi yesterday, Fiifi. No ho ye ahomka ara 'fine'". Dɛm ntsir, me kàà kyerɛɛ no dɛɛ, 'Sister girl', ɛyɛ 'fine-looking papaapa".
Oyerɛw nano na okàà de, "thank you" na onantsewee ne sisiw mu dze kɔree."
Fiifi: "Ntsir no otwaa wo "walkings" ara yie ee?"
Ato: "Me se wo dɛɛ, e, ɔsɛ wo "eye"!"

Influences of the English culture: The arrival of the 'white man'[7] on the shores of the Gold Coast had a profound effect on the population of Cape Coast. The indigenous people mingled with them and relations between European males and Ghanaian women were common, resulting in numerous births of mulattoes (children of mixed-race as they are presently known). Knowledge was shared between races and as missionaries arrived at the Gold Coast colony they succeeded in converting inhabitants of Cape Coast and surrounding areas to Christianity by building churches, schools and hospitals and the missionaries even trained nursing staff. The caucasians brought along with them not only their knowledge of science, history, theology etc. but also their mannerisms, behaviour and etiquette and this infiltrated the homes of the people of Cape Coast in one way or another. For example, parents who often spoke to their children in idiomatic expressions in the Fantse language, chided their children for displaying 'bad manners'.

---

[7] White man being either Portuguese, British, Dutch and Danish missionaries and merchants.

8.   FANTSE PROVERBS

The inhabitants of Cape Coast were taught proverbs from an early age by being spoken to proverbially and metaphorically in Fantse. Short phrases and sentences which had deeper meanings and wider references were used to explain a common experience or to render advice to young people.

For example, the saying "We talk to wise people in the form of proverbs and metaphors, not in plain language" was quite popular. The Fantse translation of this saying was: "ɔba nyansafo wobu no bɛ na wonnka no asɛm.". Many short stories narrated to children had roots in proverbs to help parents when they needed to chide the child or explain a situation or event cryptically. The following are examples of popular Fantse proverbs.

Proverb One:

English version:	A crab does not bring forth a bird
Fantse version:	"Kɔtɔ ɔnnwo anoma"
Deeper meaning:	He is like his father / Like father like son

Proverb Two:

English version:	Saying sorry does not heal wounds but soothes nerves.
Fantse version:	"Kosɛ nnsã kur nanso ɔma abodwee".
Deeper meaning:	A soft answer would not fuel one's anger.

Proverb Three:

English version:	If you disallow a friend to get to nine, then you would not arrive at ten either.
Fantse version:	"Sɛ amma wo nyɛnko enntwa akron a ɔwoso renntwa du".
Deeper meaning:	Putting impediments in the way of a friend's progress can deprive you of your own.

Proverb Four:

English version:	A child cracks the shell of a snail and not that of a tortoise.
Fantse version:	"Abofra bɔ nwa na ɔmmbɔ akyekyerɛ."
Deeper meaning:	A child does what he is capable of doing and not what is beyond him.

Proverb Five:

English version:	A child swallows "fufu" that its mouth could contain.
Fantse version:	"Abofra tsi fufu a ɔbɔkɔ n'enum".
Deeper meaning:	You should cut your coat according to your cloth.

Proverb Six:

English version:	If the back of your hand tastes good, your palm would taste better.
Fantse version:	"Wo nsa ekyir bɛyɛ wo dɛw a ɔnnkɛyɛ dɛ wo nsa ya mu."
Deeper meaning:	Blood is thicker than water.

Proverb Seven:

English version:	It is so beautiful for a maiden to clutch her breasts when running and not because they might fall.
Fantse version:	"Fɛɛfɛ na ɔyɛ fɛw dɛ ababaawa tu emirika osuo ne mpokuwa mu na nnyɛdɛ ɔbetsew atɔ bi a".
Deeper meaning:	Handsome is as handsome does.

Proverb Eight:

English version:	A child who has clean hands can eat with adults.
Fantse version:	"Sɛ abofra hu ne nsa ho hohor a ɔnnye mpanyinfo dzidzi".
Deeper meaning:	A well-mannered child can rub shoulders with adults.

Proverb Nine:

English version:	If you expect to be fed by someone then you'll sleep without food.
Fantse version:	"Sɛ edze oenyiwa to obi ne nkwan sɛn mu a ibua da".
Deeper meaning:	Self reliance is better than depending on others.

Proverb Ten:

English version:	If you are ready for marriage then you should buy your own plates.
Fantse version:	"Sɛ aso awar a nna atɔ wo mprɛtse".
Deeper meaning:	One has to be well prepared before entering marriage.

9. CAPE COAST FANTSE GENDER NAMES

Male Names

Born on	Sunday	Kwesi, Yokwesi, Yoosi, Siisi
Born on	**Monday**	Kodwo, Yokodwo, Joojo, Dwoodwo
Born on	**Tuesday**	Kɔbena, Yokɔbena, Ebow
Born on	**Wednesday**	Kweku, Yoku, Kuuku, Abeeku
Born on	**Thursday**	Ekow, Yɔkɔw, Kwaa
Born on	**Friday**	Kofi, Yoofi, Fiifi
Born on	**Saturday**	Kwamena, Ato, Yokwamena

Other name variations for males are:
Papa, Paapa, Papaa, Mpaa, Nanabanyin, Egya, Burenyi.

Female Names

Born on	Sunday	Esi, Ewuresi
Born on	**Monday**	Adwoa, Ewuradwoa
Born on	**Tuesday**	Araba, Ewurabena
Born on	**Wednesday**	Ekua, Ewurekua, Kuukua
Born on	**Thursday**	Aba, Ewuraba, Baaba
Born on	**Friday**	Efua, Ewurefua, Effie
Born on	**Saturday**	Ama, Ewurama, Adoma

Other name variations for females are:
Nana, Ewuraba Nana, Ewura Ante, Naana, Menaana, Mena, Maame, Mame, Mame Panyin, Mame Kakraba.

10. **CAPE COAST CUISINE**

Cape Coast cuisine was known to be excellent. The culinary delights of pleasant tasty food was superbly presented and would whet anyone's appetite. The process of eating either using cutlery or with one's fingers was elegantly performed by the Fantse people.

Nutritious dishes such as Palmnut soup, Groundnut soup (a.k.a peanut butter soup), plain or Light soup (a.k.a. "Nkakra" soup) were eaten with soft, lump free "fufu". Stews were prepared using fish, meat, shrimps and chicken in a variety of ways to enhance taste. A special stew (known as 'Fantse-Fantse') using minuscule tilapia from Cape Coast lagoon was a great delicacy. Boiled rice and yam, sliced kenkey and "*Etsew*" (cooked corn dough) were eaten with the stews. Jollof rice was an added tasteful delicacy. Other popular dishes were garden-egg stew, spinach (mixed with egushi[8]) stew, and egushi with shrimps. These dishes were served with root crops such as boiled cassava, boiled ripe plantain or yam. Tossed vegetable salad would be added as a side dish.

Cooking usually took all day as it was labour intensive, however cooks (housewives) managed to serve three meals a day and on time for their families. Cooking was usually done on coalpots using charcoal. Other households cooked on the mud tripod "*mbukyia*", using firewood, which was a cruder version of the coalpot. Wealthy families possessed cast-iron stoves in their kitchens which used firewood.

Pepper, tomatoes, garden-eggs and egushi were ground on a specially shaped flat stone, using a smaller one to fit into one's palms for the grinding process. Young girls were taught the grinding process by older siblings.

Dessert included fruit salad, pancake, banana fritters, and caramel custard or just sliced pineapple or other fruits which were in season.

As the demand for the culinary treats of Cape Coast cuisine increased, many enterprising women engaged in the sales of the following neatly prepared and packaged foods which they sold at various venues. Food products such as rice porridge, corn dough porridge (a.k.a. '*akwasa*' or '*mpampa*'), sugar loaves and butter bread (sold and eaten with butter or cheese) were sold to the general public. To boost the sales of the various items on sale, the women sang songs with hilarious and catchy lyrics in their loud voices to attract passers-by.

Cakes and rock buns were baked and sold as were doughnuts also known as '*Bofloat*'. "*Sweet bad*" was another popular snack which consisted of fried pastry with added sugar. '*Atwemɔ*' was a variation of sugar pastry, coconut cake and groundnut cake. A snack food

[8]   Egushi – ground dried melon seeds

known as "*Polo*" which was pastry mixed with desiccated coconut, fried or baked, sold very well especially amongst school children.

Ripe plantain was a popular basic ingredient used in the preparation of foods such as:

"Epitsi"	Ripe plantain pudding
"Esiatɔ"	Over ripe plantain baked in its skin
"Boodow ngo"	Baked ripe plantain mixed with corn dough and palm oil.
"Tatar"	Ripe plantain fritters fried in palm oil
"Krakro"	Ripe plantain mixed with corn dough and deep fried in palm oil
"Emo na eduwa"	Mashed rice and broad beans in special palm nut soup.

The dish, '*Emo na eduwa*' contained white rice which was cooked in a huge cast-iron pot and then mashed. Ground broad beans were added to the palm nut soup for thickening and it became a delicious and filling meal. The public purchased this specialised dish from certain well-known homes.

"*Boodow*" was another food product which was popular and was sold at the roadside to travellers passing through Cape Coast town. A traveller did not feel completely welcome unless they had purchased '*Boodow*' from an inhabitant of Cape Coast. '*Boodow*' was a corn-based food item which was baked and could be eaten either accompanied with fried fish for lunch or with cheese at breakfast.

Scenario at table:

Mother:	"*Araba, eat the "fufu" gently. I wish you would not slurp your soup like that*"
Daughter:	"*This groundnut soup tastes so delicious, mother and it goes down so well with the soft yam "fufu."*
Mother:	"*Table manners, my dear daughter, is the beginning of wisdom, you know*"
Daughter:	"*Alright mother, thank you*" murmured Araba.

Scenario at home: A Standard Five schoolgirl went home one day after a cookery lesson at School with a dish called "***Toad in the hole***". She proudly presented it to her mother for comments:

Daughter:	"*Ma, here is the "Toad in the hole" dish, I spoke to you about*".
Mother:	"*What is this? Was it a young toad or a wizened one? You will stop attending school if this is the kind of cooking you are being taught. I will teach you to cook better dishes at home*".
Daughter:	"*But Ma, this is a British dish, taught by an English Lady, using British ingredients!*"
Mother:	"*I think you should stick to learning to cook Cape Coast soups and stews, to please your future husband.*"

11.   EDUCATION IN CAPE COAST

11.1   Primary Education in Cape Coast

Cape Coast education standards were quite high both for boys and girls. In order to qualify to be enrolled in Infant Class One at about 6 years of age, each child had to pass a Co-ordination Test. The child was required to stretch his/her right arm over his/her head to touch their left ear.   If the child was able to do this on its own, they were admitted to Class One, but if this was not managed the child had to try again the following year.

Children walked barefoot to school. Boys wore khaki shorts and shirts and girls wore the uniforms of their chosen schools in the required colours.   From Infant Class One to Standard Three[9] lessons in reading, writing and arithmetic were taught in both the English and Fantse languages.

Example. of conversation in a classroom:

Teacher: "*Who can tell me the English name for "abow?"*
Araba: "*Please Teacher, it is "door".*
Teacher: "*Very good. What about "tokura", "ɛpon" and "egua"?"*
Ama: "*Please Teacher, "tokura" is window, "ɛpon" is table, and "egua" is "chair".*
Teacher: "*Correct! Well done Ama.   You'll go far in future with your spoken English."*

11.2   Explanation of the Education System In The Gold Coast

During this period there were no nurseries or kindergartens therefore children stayed at home until they were old enough to attend Junior School and had passed the Co-ordination Test.   Junior School began from Class 1, 2 and 3 and carried on to Standard 1, 2 and 3. The Senior School began from Standard 4 to Standard 7.   At Standard 7, each pupil sat a final examination in order to obtain the Elementary School Certificate. If it was thought that a particular pupil had the ability and was intelligent they would be put forward to sit an Intelligence Test for entry into a secondary school of their choice and upon passing the exam, a scholarship could be awarded to the pupil for entry into a secondary school. Needlework, art & crafts were taught at different levels in all schools. At the Girls Schools, from Standard 4 to Standard 7, the girls were taught Domestic Science which included Cookery, Laundry and Housewifery which was added to the school curricula.

---

9   Standard 3 is Class 3 in modern day terms.

The School Year begun in January and ended in December. The first vacation period was in June and the second vacation period was in December. During vacation some parents travelled with their children for short periods to visit relatives in nearby villages or other towns in the country.

The popular Primary Schools In Cape Coast were the following:

- Government Girls' School also known as G.G.S.
- Government Boys' School also known as G.B.S.
- Methodist Boys' School.
- St. Monica School for Girls (and for boys up to Standard Three only).
- A.M.E. Zion School. This school was co-educational.
- Roman Catholic Jubilee Boys' School:
  - numerous Catholic Schools in other neighbourhoods.
  - St. Mary's Catholic Day and Boarding School for Girls.
- Our Lady of Apostle's (OLA) Catholic Day and Boarding School for Girls.
- Our Lady of Apostle's (OLA) Catholic Training College for Girls.
- Wesley Girls' High School. (Primary Division).

11.3 Secondary Schools

The outstanding Secondary Schools in Cape Coast were the following:

- Mfantsipim.
- Wesley Girls' High School
- Holy Child Secondary School
- Adisadel College
- St. Augustine's College.

Boarding Schools: The Catholic Mission opened **Our Lady of Apostle's (OLA) Training College** for girls. **St. Mary's** day and boarding school was established for girls as well. **Our Lady of Apostle's (OLA) Day and Boarding school** also admitted girls.

Several mulatto girls were in these boarding schools and they were beautifully brought up by the nuns, who also taught them needlecraft par excellence! Many girls from all over the country sought and gained admission into these boarding schools.

11.4 EMPIRE DAY CELEBRATIONS and the youth

This was a yearly affair as well as a public holiday. The major school activity of the year was the Empire Day celebration which was held on May 24th and it was very well attended by the general public. **Empire Day** was seen as a great occasion to salute our colonial masters and in accordance with this, the British National Anthem was dutifully sang on that day. A March Past would be carried out by schoolchildren at the **Victoria Park** where stood the bust of Queen Victoria.

The uniform of black shoes and black stockings was required to be worn by girls from Standard 4 to Standard 7 who attended Government Girls' School. The turn out for the parade was impeccable both for teachers and pupils. Pupils put on their neatest uniforms while others had new ones made for the occasion. They all took great pride in their very neat appearances on Empire Day and marched beautifully to the tunes of Colonial marching songs. A prize was won by the school which marched best of all. After the parade, the children would return to their various schools for a feast or some form of refreshments which would be enjoyed by both staff and children.

12.   INTRODUCING A LIST OF PROMINENT CAPE COAST PERSONALITIES

There were several prominent citizens living in Cape Coast, during this era, especially noted because Cape Coast was known to be the cradle of the best education in the country. A few of note were the following:

Kofi Bentsi-Enchill Esq.: He was the first appointed black African managerial agent of United African Company, U.A.C. Ltd. He was a wealthy, generous and much loved gentleman who lived in his house which he called "*Adaaso*" meaning "Dream come true", situated near Adisadel College.

W.E.G. Sekyi Esq: He was a brilliant and distinguished Barrister-at-Law. He lived in his house near the Cape Coast Castle.

Sir Arku Korsah: He was a Barrister-at-Law who later became the Governor General and lived in his large house which was named "Retreat" at Turom, a suburb in Cape Coast. He later became the first Chief Justice of Ghana.

Hon. G. E. Moore: He was a renowned politician. His residence was named "Sompa" which means "Good Service", in Cape Coast.

Dr. Mercer-Ricketts: He was a well respected medical private practitioner, residing at the "Aboom" neighbourhood of the municipality.

Dr. Duker: He was a celebrated medical private practitioner, well known by many inhabitants; also resided at "Aboom".

J.E. Biney Esq. a.k.a. "Tarkwa" Biney: He was a very wealthy philanthropist whose generous handouts to needy persons were greatly appreciated.

Mr Kwabonyi Sey: He was a wealthy philanthropist. He lived in his house situated near the Castle and from his upstairs window he could see ships sailing by on the Atlantic Ocean. Mr Sey enjoyed chatting with people passing by, in his legendary unique spoken English, sprinkled with Fantse words.

A gentleman passing by his house is once known to have enquired of Mr Sey if a particular ship had sailed. He is alleged to have replied in these immortal words, "*I see the* "*wusiw kumɔɔ*", *but I never hear the bungams!*" and this was translated to mean, "*I see the thick smoke-stack emissions but I have not heard the booming of the ships cannons yet*".

A few distinguished ladies who provided outstanding good works within the Cape Coast municipality were the following.

"Ewuraba Town Council", also known as Madam Marian Wood, was the first lady Cape Coast Town Councillor. She was one of five distinguished ladies who founded the "Guild of the Good Shepherd", in the Anglican Church, and was a much respected pillar in the church.

"Ewuraba Hostel", as Mrs Dalrymple Hayfron was affectionately called, operated a hostel and sewing school for girls. Some of the young girls living in the hostel attended primary schools as well.

Mrs Faustina Daniels popularly called "Auntie Faustie", also ran a hostel and sewing school. It was well patronised, for her meticulous sewing of wedding dresses and ballroom dancing gowns.

Mrs Mary Arthur–Hughes, popularly called "Teacher Mary", taught at Wesley Girls High School, primary division. She was an excellent pianist and housewife.

Mrs Mary Arthur was a hardworking midwife of high repute. She made several home deliveries of bouncing babies, and went on her daily visits to expectant mothers, assiduously.

Mrs Jessie Bannerman popularly called "Auntie Jessie" was a smart dedicated midwife, well known and highly respected in the municipality of Cape Coast.

Some of these prominent personalities who resided in Cape Coast were also immersed in politics. The Fantse people had always had appetites for decent political discussions on issues leading to better nation building and good governance.

---

13.   **COMMERCIAL TRADING**

Kotokuraba Road and Commercial Street were the main shopping centres in Cape Coast. The United African Company Ltd (U.A.C.) dominated the trading scene. Many mothers who were venturing into the retail trade, acquired "pass books" which were required in order to collect goods from U.A.C. on credit. The goods were then sold on to customers for an ample profit and in that way, the women were able to provide an income to help their families. The popular goods that were for sale were Wax print textiles and tobacco.

A group emerged of mainly elderly, illiterate women known as "*Konkosifo*" who engaged in petty trading of all kinds of goods from their homes. The goods were kept under their iron bedsteads and were sold in small amounts at a time, thus cunningly creating unnecessary shortages.

Another group were also known as "*Bagyirbanyi*". The term was applied to a well-to-do stylish woman engaged in brisk business. The Bagyirbanyis connived with a few handsome young Managers-under-Training at the larger trading establishments to supply them with more than their fair share of essential commodities which the ladies would then retail for a tidy profit resulting in them becoming extremely rich. These women dressed well having accumulated several expensive gold trinkets – an indication of their wealth. As a reward for this deal, the Bagyirbanyis would reciprocate by sending special tasty dishes, cakes and fragrant butter bread to the offices of the young Managers.

Scenario at the market:
Esi met Mansa in front of Anaafo market near the U.A.C. Head Office one afternoon.
"*Eh! Mansa, have you heard, Mame Ekua's bedroom was searched last Friday by the police, on a tip off?*" Esi excitedly said to her friend.
"*No! Tell me more, and what did they find?*" Mansa enquired.
Esi narrated, "*Cartons and cartons of sardines, Tate sugar, condensed milk and several bundles of tobacco hidden under her fabulous bedstead. The police carried everything away in a truck while people stared and jeered*".
Mansa remarked, "*Oh dear! Mame Ekua is such a kind-hearted woman but it is not fair to hoard goods thus creating a shortage which means prices will soar. I hope she will be dealt with leniently, though*".
"*I hope so too*", Esi replied.
And on that note both girls walked briskly into the market.

13.1   Nana Memen

"Nana Memen" was an elderly illiterate woman of substance and was a well-known wealthy "Konkosinyi" who also sold essential commodities.   The literal translation of her name was "Grandma Red".   She lived in a compound house with several illiterate maidservants (or house girls) from poor families who were under an apprenticeship. Grandma Red organised to cook large amounts of a popular cooked bean dish known as "Abɔbɔe".   At 6.00 a.m. the maidservants would carry the cooked beans in large black pots on their heads to the various communities for sale to the public.   At midday the girls would be back home to render their accounts to Grandma Red.   The girls worked hard but were not paid, however, they were fed and clothed.   At the end of two years service, the girls would be able to return to their individual villages with Ten Pounds Sterling in cash (a considerable amount in those days) to start their own business.   They would also be given a metal trunk (known as "air-tight") which contained six pieces of wax print cloth, headscarves, a pair of native sandals and a pair of gold earrings.   The option was given for them to stay on until a suitor came to ask for their hand in marriage, if they preferred. Nana Memen treated the girls well and many were reluctant to return to the village (in spite of their gifts) and instead remained, got married and continued working for Nana Memen.

13.2   Other Traders:

Lagosians from Nigeria were experts in petty retail trading and they had stalls and shops all over town, selling almost everything from provisions to pills.   Other traders carried large wooden trays on their heads which were full of household items, such as pairs of scissors, penknives, safety pins, packets of blades and anything they could lay their hands on.   They were dubbed "*Pampamu Store*" which literally means "store carried on the head" in the Fantse language.   The men could be found trading on the streets or anyplace where people gathered.   They would also go from house to house selling their wares and if there was an item they did not immediately have, they would obtain it elsewhere and return the next day with the required item for sale. Trading everywhere was carried out in a leisurely manner and people were quite satisfied with fairly reasonable profits.   The "get-rich-quick" syndrome was unknown during this period.

Indians, Lebanese and Syrian traders opened fancy goods stores; such as Bombay Bazaar and Chellarams where household goods were sold.   The auto spare parts shops and businesses were operated by Syrian and Lebanese persons.   There were no supermarkets as such, but small shops sold many different goods.

14.   HEALTH INSPECTORS

Health Inspectors had the distinguished job of visiting each home to ascertain its cleanliness for themselves in every neighbourhood. An assistant health officer armed with a soup ladle (of all things) would collect a sample of stored water for drinking, to see if it was contaminated or perfect for domestic use. If standards were unsatisfactory, the head of the household would be put before the courts and made to pay a fine if found guilty and this resulted in the cleanliness in most neighbourhoods being satisfactory. There were however, some petty thieves and fraudsters who posed as health workers and visited homes, charged a few shillings, and then promised to have charges, which had been brought against some heads of families, dropped. Needless to say charges were never dropped as these fraudsters did not work for the Courts. Armed robbery was thankfully unknown in Cape Coast in that era.

15.   REPORT ON OTHER ETHNIC GROUPS EXISTING IN CAPE COAST

The other ethnic groups who lived within the Fantse communities were very hospitable and they learnt to speak the Fantse language well in order to integrate with the locals. Some of them rented rooms in homes where, by association, they gradually acquired the genteel mannerisms of the Fantse people of Cape Coast. The Nzemas, Ahantas, Sierra Leonians and Liberians were ethnic groups who were in the minority in the municipality.

Hausa inhabitants: The dominant ethnic group were the Hausas (who came from the northern regions of Ghana). They lived around the Kotokuraba market area and were mostly Muslims, earning their living as butchers selling fresh meat in the market during the day and delicious kebab[10] at night. As part of their culture, circumcision of baby boys was performed (sometimes under quite unhygienic conditions) by Hausa men referred to as "*Wanzams*". In some cases, some elderly Hausa women practised female circumcision on Muslim baby girls, resulting on occasion in unfortunate circumstances.

Ewe inhabitants: The Ewe group (a tribe who originate from the Volta Region of Ghana), lived in rented rooms in any neighbourhood of their choice. The men folk were very hardworking and went from house to house performing laundry duties such as washing & ironing of clothes (using flat irons) for a small fee and this was their main occupation. Their wives engaged mainly in producing Gari (processed grains derived from the cassava plant), which was highly patronised by secondary students in boarding schools because storage was easy and gari was quite a filling meal for hungry students. As a result of the popularity of gari as a staple food, one particular Fantse household in Cape Coast learned

---

[10]   Meat cooked with delicious hot spices and pepper on a stick over an open fire.

the art of making gari and became specialists with people travelling from far afield to purchase their product.

Ga inhabitants: The men of the Gâ community were usually employed as civil servants. The wives of the Gâ men indulged in petty trading of assorted goods and were called, "***Mame Nkran***" (a variation of the pronunciation of Accra spoken in vernacular).

Nigerian inhabitants: Many Nigerians lived and traded in Cape Coast. The Nigerian women had stalls where they lived, in any neighbourhood of their choice, selling almost everything they believed the inhabitants would readily buy, products as diverse as salt and sardine. The women became known as "***Mame Alata***" – a colloquial name for Nigerians in Cape Coast.

16.   FANTSE TRADITIONS AND CUSTOMS

16.1   **Sex**

Sex was a taboo subject and it was not discussed in any circles but was referred to in idiomatic Fantse. Young girls below the age of 13 wore beads round their waists and they also wore a special long red cloth between the thighs covering the genital area, and held in place by the beads. This "Red Turkey Cloth" or R.T.C. as it was known in Cape Coast, was washed daily and hung out to dry. Some of the beads worn were of dazzling colours, that looked very attractive on slim waists.

16.2   **Celebration of First Menstruation**

At **Puberty**, a young girl began to broaden at particular parts of the body, and the breasts became enlarged. It was deemed time to delicately mention menstruation or the monthly periods to her as a fact of life. This information was imparted by older siblings or a relative and even peers at school. Mothers were too embarrassed to educate their daughters about sex. In cryptic chosen Fantse sentences, one would be told one was on the way towards motherhood soon. Girls were taught about extra general cleanliness of their bodies which needed to be followed at this particular time. They were taught how to use the juice of a sliced lime fruit as a deodorant for any body odour.

After this talk the young girl would be carefully watched by members of her family and when the event did occur it was quietly celebrated by all members at home and the extended family. On the day, כtכ is specially prepared early in the morning for the young girl's delight. It is a celebratory dish of mashed yam gently mixed in flavoured palm oil and decorated with boiled eggs. After a short prayer, an elderly female family member would touch the young girl's lips thrice with the כtכ food. The rest of the people in the household would then join in the feasting of this special food dish.

Menstruation was usually experienced after the age of fifteen however the onset of menstruation seems to become earlier with each generation due to better diet and better health care of children.

In the villages, some months after puberty, illiterate young girls were "outdoored" or marketed as it were, to attract male suitors.

This was how the girls were dressed:

- Each girl wore a "*Tekua*" hair style on their heads. The "Tekua" was shaped like an inverted pot, made with horse hair, greased into shape with car grease and Vaseline, and covered with a special black silky thread called "*Abyssinia*";

- The "Tekua" was then decorated with several gold brooches, and long pins of various designs. The garments worn were made of embossed silk cloth and locally woven Kente cloths.

- Necklaces of Aggrey beads and a long gold chain would be worn around her neck. Some more Aggrey beads and gold bracelets were worn around the wrists, and beads were placed on their legs just below both the knee caps.

- Solid gold earrings were placed in the girl's ear lobes to make her look more adorned. She would then parade majestically on the streets projecting her suitability and readiness for marriage. On this occasion the adorned girl would usually be chaperoned by another girl, also gorgeously attired but sporting a much less decorated "Tekua" and wearing a small gold necklace.

After that celebration the young woman was expected to be on her best behaviour until a suitor came along.

Scenario: Conversation after a Puberty Outdooring

"*Mansa has been blooming since her outdooring. Did you take a good look at the ornaments adorning her "tekua" the other day?*" Adwoa commented to her friend Effie.

Effie added, "*They were a fabulous real gold collection! She is such a nice person. I wish a respectable young bachelor will soon ask for her hand in marriage.*"

Fathers and male relatives privately lectured their son and adolescent boys about wet dreams and the young men were explicitly taught the facts of life. Other young boys discussed the subject with their friends and older brothers.

16.3   Celebrations of a Birth

After the child is born and bathed, it is wrapped in swaddling cloths only, and not in baby dress. This was done for the first eight days. As a result of the high infant mortality rate in these years, the baby was kept indoors to see whether it would survive or not. The infant's bed was made with some old clean clothing folded like a cushion on the mother's bed and the child was breast fed.

16.4   The Outdooring:

After the eighth day, respective extended families would gather for the naming ceremony. The baby, in white chemise (or vest) would be wrapped in a white sheet or towel and would be carried out by a senior male member of the family who would make a speech formally welcoming the child into the family. He would then address the baby.

An ancestral name would be chosen together with the appropriate Fantse gender name. A baby boy born on Sunday would be called Kwesi, and may be also called Boadu, after an ancestor, so his name would then be known as "Kwesi Boadu." A cup containing water, and another one containing Schnapps (both clear liquids) would be placed beside the elderly male holding the baby. He would dip his finger into the alcoholic drink and touch the baby's tongue whilst repeating these words:

"*Kwesi, sɛ ese nsã a, nna nsã a.*" This was repeated three times. The same process was repeated with the water saying three times:

"*Kwesi, sɛ ese nsu a, nna nsu a*", and the words translated meant "Kwesi, let your yea be yea, and your nay, nay."

Gifts in cash were accepted by the mother. This occasion would be the first time the baby would have been brought out into the daylight sun. If it is a boy, circumcision would be performed on the eighth day by a Hausa man known as a "Wanzam" and precautions were taken to ensure hygienic conditions however this was not always the case so many frightened mothers left circumcision to be performed later by a surgeon when the boys grew up. If the child was a girl, her ear lobes would be pierced by a midwife or an elderly trained woman.

16.5   Celebration of the Birth Of Twins

The birth of twins was joyfully celebrated. Identical twin boys, identical twin girls, and non-identical twins had the same naming ceremonies, with marked variations for twins only.

On the eighth day, after both babies had been bathed, they would be smeared with white clay. Special five beads called "*Abam Kofi*" were threaded on yellow coloured raffia, and tied round the left wrists which signified their special status in the family. The five special beads were of the following colours: Blue, Gold, White, Black, Red. The "*Abam*" wristlet identified twins and the siblings born after them. It was supposed to have some magical powers given to them by a god or goddess. Identical twins were much admired and sometimes the twins turned out to be very mischievous.

Gender names for twins were; "Ata Panyin" for the first of the twins to be born. "Ata Kakra" was the name given to the second twin born. If the female twin was born on a Monday she would be called "Adwoa Ata Panyin". They could also be called just plain "Panyin and Kakra" or Kodwo Ata Kakra (if male) and Adwoa Ata Panyin (if female).

The child who was born <u>after twins</u> was always called "Tawia". A female child would be called "Efua Tawia" and a male child "Kofi Tawia" if both were born on a Friday.

The child born <u>after</u> "Tawia" was named "Nyankomabo". The next child born after Nyankomabo would be called "Abam". All these children were entitled to wear the special "abam" wristlets.

16.6   The Yearly Twin Festival

Twins and any siblings after them, celebrated the Yearly Festival in August and September when new yams had been harvested. On the Festival Day, the twins as well as siblings born after twins, would be bathed with special herbs early in the morning and smeared with white clay all over their bodies. New clothes, preferably white clothes, would be worn by the children, and the celebratory dish, "כɔtɔ" would be eaten by all. "Abam" wristlets were worn by them and they would go round visiting relatives and friends to show off their new clothes and wristlets and each child received gifts from well-wishers.

16.7   "Kwasama" Births

Repeated infant deaths (which happened to the same mother) was known as "Kwasama" which translated to mean 'return to be born again'. After a third or fourth occurrence of such deaths, marks would be made at both temples near the eyes of the baby with a sharp knife, or a blade. Similar marks would be inflicted at right and left sides of the mouth, jaw and other parts of the body, before the dead baby was buried. At the next birth; if the newborn baby would have the same marks at the same places on its body and then survive, it was alleged to have been re-born. Such children were easily identified in the communities by their facial and body marks, and queer names.

"Kwasama" babies were given queer names at naming ceremonies such as "Dɔnkɔ", meaning slave; "Sumina", meaning garbage heap; "Wangar", meaning person from unknown ancestry.

16.8   Guidance towards naming other siblings in the family

A first born child was always known as "Abakan" A second born child was called "Manu". The third of three sons in a row was "Mensa" and the third of three daughters in a row was always known as "Mansa".

If Two boys were followed by a girl; she would be called "**Akyere** ".
If Two girls were followed by a boy; he would be called "**Twentɔ**".
The Fourth boy in a row would be called "**Annan**".
The Fourth girl in a row would be "**Maanan**".
The Sixth female child could be called "**Esia** or "**Esiaba**"
The Seventh child was named "**Esuon**".
The Eighth child was "**Awotwe**"
The Ninth child was called "**Nkrumah**"
The Tenth child was named "**Badu**".

When a mother delivered a tenth baby, a ram was slaughtered and delicious meals prepared for a celebration. The mother would eat the meal sitting on a "Badu Mat" surrounded by family, friends and well wishers.

16.9   The Custom of Traditional Engagement

A bachelor, ready for marriage would inform his parents of his intentions and would ask his father to request the hand of the young woman he had been admiring for some time. The first act to be performed would be the "Knocking ceremony" held at the woman's Father's house, where a bottle of Schnapps and four pounds (£4.00) cash would have to be presented. A day would then be set aside and agreed upon for the full ceremony. The following would be the required list for the whole ceremony, from the male's family to the female's family:

	DEED REQUIRED TO BE PERFORMED	FEE
1.	Knocking fee and one bottle of Schnapps	£4.00
2.	Door opening or Appreciation	£2.00
3.	Asking of hand, one bottle of Schnapps and cash	£5.00
4.	Acceptance	£2.00
5.	Donation towards Bride's Father's Tobacco	£10.00
6.	Bride's Mother's "Tamboba" (which literally means "for her toils")	£10.00
7.	"Tsir Nsà" or Head Drink Engagement Ring, Bible	£5.00
8.	Dowry: Cash, Clothing, Assorted drinks etc.	£50.00
9.	Money donated to Brothers-in-Law	£5.00
10.	Thanks "Aseda"	£5.00

An amount of about one hundred and five pounds (£105.00) would have been spent. A Bible and ring for the maiden, sealed everything. The spokespersons for the male delegation and that of the female side traded jokes and spoke lovingly of the attributes of the bachelor and the spinster in witty idiomatic Fantse.

The young woman would be referred to as "*A Rose of Sharon in a beautiful flower garden that is to be uprooted and transplanted into a joyous environment*". The young man would also be referred to as "*A handsome and dignified personality and a desirable man with whom any one would just love to have children*". More hilarious lyrics in song would have the company present in stitches.

The family of the young girl would provide refreshments for relatives and guests who witnessed the ceremonies. Female participants would each receive a wristlet of white beads as a token for being at the function. A male elder from the delegation would be given a bottle of Schnapps to return home and report back to the bachelor's Head of Family and his own father, of an assignment well carried out. Members of both families, friends and guests were courteously introduced. Everyone would have a jolly good time and the merrymaking could continue from late morning to late afternoon.

Three months or more after the engagement, the "Tekua" would be worn on the head of the young woman who had been engaged. More gold ornaments would adorn the "Tekua" and long ropes of "Aggrey Beads" and long gold chains would be worn round the neck. Heavy gold earrings, beads and gold wristlets, would be worn by the bride to be. She would put on rich embossed silk clothing, changing this clothing daily for some weeks. Once suitably dressed, the bride to be, accompanied by two modestly dressed maidens, one on her left, and the other on her right would go visiting in town to show the world that an engagement had actually taken place. On such occasions, very wealthy women placed orders for the intricate gold trinkets on display on the girls, which were hired out for such events. The goldsmiths who carried out such works, were very efficient and competent and their work was in great demand.

16.10 Customary Marriages following an Engagement

When the engagement celebrations are over, for about three months thereafter the husband-to-be would have set a date for his bride to come live with him. This usually took place on a bright moonlit night and around six o'clock in the evening on that day; close relatives would go along with the bride, singing and carrying different cooked foods in huge highly polished brass bowls. The brides clothes would be placed in a set of trunks (a.k.a. metal suitcases) and carried over to the husband's house. A dimly lit lantern would be carried along by the small procession and as they walk along the road, they continue to sing. On their arrival, a spokeswoman of the group would explain their mission to the gentleman and some friends of his who had gathered there waiting for the bride to arrive.

After trading some more witty remarks and pleasant jokes, refreshments would be served. Delicious Cape Coast cuisine was served buffet style. After the buffet dinner, the husband would see all the women off at the door; and then would subtly ask his own friends to depart too, as he has some personal entertainment to attend to. They would all agree and merrily leave him alone with his wife. A wife was to be found a virgin on her wedding night and therefore the next day, after the event, a bottle of hard liquor with a piece of calico tied at the neck was sent to the wife's parents. This gesture said it all: "She was a virgin. Congratulations!" The wife would have brought untold embarrassment to her parents if found otherwise. Three months or so later, a trusted friend of the wife could be asked to spy on her friend in order to look for early signs of pregnancy.

SCENARIO AT THE BRIDE'S PARENTS' HOUSE:

Husband: "*How is it, dear wife, has our daughter been spitting? Have her breasts enlarged?*" enquired Mr Ashun anxiously, as the couple retired to their bedroom one evening.

Wife: "*Not yet, my lord, let's be patient and give them more time.*" Replied Mama Ashun quietly.

Husband: "*If you say so, dear wife, but I'll be a good father to go and pluck my daughter back home without delay if no signs of pregnancy appear, having lived with her husband for nearly a year now. What do you say, Woman?*"

Wife: "*Patience, my good husband patience is the key. God in His wisdom and in His own time will grant us the adoring grandchild we crave for, I'm sure,*" whispered Mother Ashun. "*Goodnight and sound sleep*", she added softly.

As a general rule, if after a while, there was no sign of pregnancy, the Father of the Bride could ask for the return of his daughter.

16.11 Holy Matrimony

The educated Christian ladies in Cape Coast preferred to celebrate the solemnization of their marriage in church with all the trappings such as, wedding invitations, the wedding gown, the wedding cake, an adequate reception and a honeymoon, after the ceremonies. At such wedding receptions, party food would be served in abundance along with a variety of drinks and sweets. Gate-crashers took the opportunity to attend as well.

SCENARIO: Gatecrashers discuss tactics the day before a wedding:

"*Yɔkɔw, we shall be at the reception of the wealthy Mr Fynn's daughter tomorrow afternoon at the Town Hall*". Mark stated to his younger brother, Yɔkɔw.

"*Have we been invited?*" enquired Yɔkɔw.

Mark replied, "*Who will know? There will be several gate-crashers. You just slip one clean white pillow case under your shirt. We shall arrive early and hover around?*"

"*And why the pillow case?*" Yɔkɔw nervously asks his elder brother.

"*Our share of the goodies will be stored in the pillow case as quickly as possible. Two of the many young men who will be serving, are my friends. They will cleverly pour whole trays of goodies into the pillow case you will whip out from under your shirt on cue, with a slight nod from me, trust me!*" answered Mark.

"*There will be many similar trays and several people will be grabbing goodies into all sorts of bags and containers, laughing and enjoying themselves,* Mark continued, *so no one will even notice us as we make our way silently out of the hall, return home and enjoy the booty. Okay?*"

"*Right you are, my brother, you are an absolute genius!*" Yɔkɔw said excitedly.

The festivities continue for several days until the bride and bridegroom depart for their honeymoon which would probably be in Sekondi, Takoradi or any neighbouring town. It seems a young adolescent's lifestyle in Cape Coast was charming and carefree.

16.12   Customary rituals performed at a Demise

The end of life, death, was always sad whether it occurs naturally, as in old age or suddenly as a result of an accident or fatally by terminal disease. When it did occur in the family and it was certified by a medical practitioner, the body was removed from the bed to the floor on a mat and covered. Closest next of kin were quickly sent for to straighten out the body and to prepare to embalm in customary fashion: "*Kaadow*" (a.k.a. whitewash) was poured down the throat. Milton could also be used in this instance.

Other notified relatives would then gather in the house and funeral arrangements would be made. Burial took place within three days or slightly more as there were no fridges to preserve the bodies. A Wake was kept as the mildly adorned body in a white shroud was laid on a bed. Many people attend such a Wake, most of them cried, others wailed till dawn whilst chewing cola nuts to keep them awake. Close relatives put rings on the fingers of the corpse signifying parting forever. A small amount of money was put inside the coffin because it was believed the dead person would use the monies to pay the toll in order to cross the river to the other side of the universe. After burial, a date would be set for a family gathering for the final obsequies which would be held a month to three months later.

"*Nkaansa*" would be sent to widows or widowers and in-laws. These monies was to remind them of their obligations to the family at such a sad time. Each amount received was doubled by ten percent or more according to the financial status of the family member.

16.13   "FIA" – Demise of a Child

"*Fia*" occurred when a child was the first to pass away. The funeral was not supposed to be elaborate at all. Whitish mourning cloth was worn. The family would "sit-in-state" to receive mourners, however donations were not announced but were put in a basin obscurely placed in a corner. Mourners were not expected to stay long at the funeral home as superstition demands in order that this unfortunate event is not repeated within the same family.

16.14   "TƆFO" – Fallen Victims

The death of a victim by car accident or through childbirth made him or her an "Otɔfo" meaning a fallen victim. The latter was deemed a great family calamity. Whilst an accident victim would be laid out on a bed for wake-keeping, the childbirth victim if it did not survive, was placed upright in a big chair in a white shroud. In certain clans, if a mother died giving birth to a stillborn child, the infant would be placed on her knee to be buried together. Certain clans would not even consider bringing the bodies of such victims home for wake keeping. However, as was the norm, from the hospital mortuary the body was brought to the gate of the deceased's house for a short while, to be viewed by mourners and then quickly removed for burial. Funeral rites were very simple and quick to avoid repetition, as superstition demanded.

16.15   Widowhood

The widow immediately became a target of animosity from her late husband's family. The widow was required to bathe at dawn and early evening and was not to be seen to talk too much nor was she allowed to handle money during the mourning period.

Mourning clothes had to be worn daily and were usually black. The widow wore raffia round her neck and was required to sit on a low stool or on the floor and had to spend the night lying on the floor preferably on a mat. She was never left alone and a family member was by her side at all times. Each night, at midnight, the widow was required to carry a pot of garbage or charcoal fire on her head to the beach where she would throw her load into the sea. On the way to the beach she would shout "*Wonnhyia o!*" translated to mean "I am not to be seen/met by anyone". Ill luck might befall anyone who did meet up with the widow so everyone avoided her. The widow then bathed in the sea. This act was to ward off the spirit following her around. Some widows maintained that they would see the spirit of their late husband who gave them comforting messages. In those days the widow was fortunate if she was not thrown out of the marital home.

Widowers had a much easier life. They were not expected to stay on the stool all day and they could wear their normal clothes and sit comfortably on a chair. The widowers could even go to bed during wake-keepings. At midnight, the widower would be required to tie his deceased wife's cloth around his waist and he would then be taken to the seaside to have a dip in the ocean to ward off his wife's ghost which may be following him around.

16.16   Clothes worn at Funerals

Black cloth was usually worn on the funeral day. The Widow or Widower and children of the deceased and other family members tied a piece of cloth around their wrists to distinguish them from mourners. They paraded round the town wailing bitterly with their hands on their heads to signify grief. Their arms and cheeks were decorated with red mud. Women would sing dirges and bang sticks together in order to create a large noise.

Aggrey beads and gold were placed around the neck of the deceased person if they were from the royal family or were particularly wealthy. In such an event, a full grown heifer was carefully bridled and held, and it led the procession of mourners.

16.17   Organisation of Funerals

The family head sit-in-state surrounded by other members of the family on the maternal side. A **clan emblem** is displayed on a special pole. Some clan names in Cape Coast are the following:

1.   Royal Kona Ebiradze Paramount Stool Family of Oguaa.
      Emblem : Eko - **Bison**
2.   Anona clan. Ekow - **Parrot**
3.   Twidan clan. Sebo - **Leopard**
4.   Nsona clan. Akonkoran - **Crow**
5.   Abadze clan. Bodom - **Dog**
6.   Kona clan. Eko - **Bison**
7.   Adwendadze. Awenadze - **Lion**

There would be a large gathering and mourning clothes would be worn. The widow or widowers family present their "*Esiadze*" - which consists of money, Schnapps and soft drinks. Descendants of the deceased would follow suit with the same form of presentation. Donations from family members, extended family and friends and well wishers follow after that. Refreshments are served such as "*Ahe*" (a corn drink), minerals, beer and palm wine.

A Memorial service is held on the Sunday following the burial and another family gathering is called.

"Mbo-mbo" custom: Monday saw the **"Mbo-mbo" custom** being performed which is the act of family members going round the town to thank those who had donated large sums of money to help defray funeral costs and/or food, to help feed relatives and visitors who had travelled from towns or villages situated outside Cape Coast.

At the family gathering after the burial, accounts are examined and settled. Each family member pays a levy to help defray expenses. Members of the family who lent money to ensure proper arrangements were made, receive their monies back and any other loans raised to defray costs are paid off. All necessary accounting is to be settled such as payments for cost of food and drink, cost of the hall (if used), cost of all decorations, cost of the burial plot and the cost of the designated Family Funeral Cloth supplied to all members of the immediate family etc.

CHAPTER II

PRE-WAR YEARS: MID 30'S TO THE DECLARATION OF WORLD WAR II (1939)

CHAPTER II
PRE-WAR YEARS: MID 30'S TO THE DECLARATION OF WORLD WAR II (1939)

17.   ADOLESCENT REMINISCENCES OF GROWING UP IN CAPE COAST

Social aspects:

There were a few drop-outs living in Cape Coast town. Some of the female drop-outs travelled to Takoradi (which was a bustling harbour town) to seek their fortunes. Most of the drop-outs got jobs as telephone operators working for the Post and Telegraphs Corporation. Others who stayed in Cape Coast traded in essential commodities. The illiterate girls sold various items in the markets. Male drop-outs and other boys who could not attend school for financial and other reasons became artisans, specialising as carpenters, blacksmiths and goldsmiths. Others became fully-fledged shoemakers and masons. Young men who had put maid servants in the family way and bolted to join the army or indeed had unceremoniously left Cape Coast, were known as "Abongo Boys".

A typical conversation between two girls of this era:

"*Look, look at this pair of beautiful earrings my brother Kofi has made for me*" announced Adwoa to her friend Efua.

"*Really!*" exclaimed Efua. "*They are lovely. Can you please ask him to make a similar pair for me?*"

"*He is only an apprentice artisan you know, that is what you said, when I introduced him to you the other day!*" remarked Adwoa.

"*I am sorry. I have changed my mind, he really is an expert*" Efua said quietly.

"*Alright, I shall ask him, as you are my best friend.*" Replied Adwoa.

"*Thank you very much Adwoa, thank you*", said Efua joyfully.

Extra-curricular activities: Elementary school activities held later on in the year were; singing competitions, sports competitions and concerts. These competitions were absolutely hilarious and most enjoyable. Many children got to know which schools other pupils attended through these activities. Brownies and Girl Guides was established for girls, and Wolf Cubs and Boy Scouts was designated for boys and these were enthusiastically patronised.

Teachers: Even though the teachers were poorly paid as usual, they taught extremely well to produce brilliant scholars who gained admission into the civil service, after passing the Standard Seven examination with distinction and became very efficient hard working civil servants. Teachers were competent and dedicated and were highly respected in the communities. Most girls went on to train as teachers, nurses, midwives and dressmakers though very few could attend secondary school, or were even allowed to and as a result many of them married early and bore children almost immediately.

The advent of radio: By the middle of the nineteen thirties a national broadcasting station was installed in Cape Coast, much to the delight of the citizens. School children were encouraged to listen to the News programmes and pupils from various primary schools would go to the local station, accompanied by their teachers to broadcast stories and sing songs. These broadcasts were enjoyed by the youth and adults alike.

The Coronation: The coronation of **King George VI**[11] came two years later. The population of Cape Coast joined in the Government festivities and thousands of school children received a gift of a cup each with the British Royal couple's photograph engraved on them. Assorted toffees and biscuits were shared out to all the schools making the school children extremely happy! News about Princess Elizabeth and her sister Princess Margaret Rose, was avidly read. Life in Cape Coast appeared prosperous and calm.

Earthquake of 1939: Suddenly, without warning, the 1939 earthquake struck, bringing panic, disaster and ruin. Many buildings collapsed, killing and maiming many inhabitants. The Red Cross (a charity organisation) gave a helping hand and calmed people's fears while many wealthy people also helped the needy. Typical of the nature of Cape Coast, a pop song about this disaster soon became the latest hit, and so even among the rubble; people danced some "*Konkoma*" steps, especially the vigorous adolescent youth.

World War II: World War II was declared the same year as the earthquake; shattering the sedate lifestyle of the citizens of Cape Coast Tunes of romantic songs which were usually whistled by young people going for evening strolls in a calm and relaxed manner were abruptly changed.

Romantic songs such as the following were whistled:

- "*Getting sentimental, wants to bill and coo?*".
- "*Give me five minutes more, only five minutes more, let me stay let me stay in your arms.*"
- "*Gonna take a sentimental journey*".

Many more songs changed overnight into war songs which the soldiers used to march with. Fathers, husbands, sons and male relatives joined the army while many others were conscripted to fight alongside the Allied Forces against Germany and in the Far East. School children were made to join in the war effort. Palm kernels were cracked by them and teachers collected the nuts from the pupils to extract oil for soap making. Scarves and blankets were knitted for the soldiers who had been sent abroad. School children sang the army songs with gusto, not having the slightest idea how people in general were suffering.

---

[11]   King George VI is the father of the present Queen of Britain, Queen Elizabeth II.

They sang songs with words such as:

> "*Give to it Spitfire's fund.*
> *Give to it whatever you can spare.*
> *Whether a mite or a pound.*
> *Give! And that will help us to win the war.*
> *Give to it Spitfire's fund.*
> *Give! For our freedom is at stake.*
> *And so, let's spit! Spit! Spit! Spit!*
> *Spit on Hitler's face and that will help us to win the war*!"

The Spitfire aeroplanes were shown on newsreels at cinemas. Letters of encouragement were written by pupils to unknown heroic pilots and soldiers overseas, whose addresses were supplied by colonial officials.

18.   FANTSE MUSIC IN THE '30S AND '40S

The lyrics of Cape Coast Fantse music were mainly commentaries about recent events such as earthquakes, World War II, the first aeroplane crash and the sad passing away of a much-loved paramount chief of Cape Coast, **Nana Mbra III**. Funeral dirges were the specialities of some female church groups and they were to be noticed at such sad events.

In the absence of any topical events, Fantse romantic songs were created by the musicians for dancing "Highlife". "Highlife" is the traditional music with words in vernacular which has an upbeat modern rhythm singularly native only to The Gold Coast. Nicknames of well-known persons were also set to music and these were full of innuendos and insinuations which the victims were unable to defend. Big bands such as the "Cape Coast Sugar Babies", played popular Highlife tunes at ballroom dances for adults to enjoy.

The youth sang songs and choruses around the town such as:

English: "My affection is unparalleled for this young man, this gentleman, this heart-string, with all my love.

Fantse: "Otse dɛn ara mpo a me dɔ wɔ no mu oo papabi. Obi n'abroba me dɔ wɔ no mu oo papabi. Obi n'ahoma tsea me dɔ wɔ no mu oo papabi".

A hit tune was sang by the citizens of Cape Coast soon after the earthquake disaster in 1939:

English: Mother left hurriedly leaving her child behind at the onset of the earthquake. Husband left his wife behind while fleeing the earthquake not realising the Almighty was just turning round.

Fantse: "Daano asaase wosow ena sɔre a, oegya ne ba hɔ. Daano asaase wosow ikun sɔre a oegya a yer hɔ.

        Chorus sung 3 times: Saana asaase wura;

        Chorus sung 3 times: ɔse orutwa no ho kakra. Motwa konkoma a maabɔ fa mu".

Tune dedicated to the memory of Nana Mbra III. The song was sang throughout the painful period of many months of mourning, in hushed voices:

English: "Let us whisper sombrely the sad death of Nana Mbra III, not knowing if he might return."

Fantse: "Nana Mbra III owu yɛ yaw oo. Wɔnkã no berɛberɛw sɛ ɔbeba a ye nyim."

Musicians came out with a song of praise and thanks to President Franklin D. Roosevelt of the United States of America when he ordered the American army to join the Allied Forces to fight the Germans in World War II. The same tune was used to sing both the Fantse words and English words which schoolchildren sang alternately at functions with gusto where they were joyously applauded:

English: "Thanks Roosevelt, it is well of you for the way you are helping us to carry on. You will see the British Empire smiling through when these dark and stormy days are gone.

And Franklin by the way, please convey our congratulations to the folks in USA. We are saying thanks, Mr Roosevelt, we are proud of you for the way you are helping us to carry on!"

Fantse: "Yɛ da wo ase America hɔn panyin dɛ ereboa hɛn ma yaakõ yeedzi kunyim.

Eko kɛse yi sɛ onya na ɔbɔ adze a, ibohu dɛ English aborɔfo nyinaa abɔmu reserew ae! Fa hɛn nkanfo ma wo man, yɛserɛw, wɔ aber a iritu akɔ Americanfo kurom mu hɔn. Yɛreka no dɛ, yɛ da wo ase America hɔn panyin dɛ ereboa hɛn ma yaakõ yeedzi kunyim!"

On one occasion, an aeroplane crashed at Saltpond beach, a few miles from Cape Coast during World War II. Many people rushed to the scene. The musicians produced a song concerning that event:

English: A red, white and blue coloured French aeroplane V7809 crash-landed at Saltpond beach. Many people rushed to the scene to have a look. Its upper wires showed the white man should be congratulated for manufacturing such a good thing.

Fantse: French aeroplane V seven eight O nine (V7809). No ho red, white and blue osi mpoano wɔ mbasen nkɔhwɛ. Wɔnhwɛ no sor "wires" ahoma. Iyi dze burenyi ɔayɛ adze a oye." "Wɔnhwɛ edɔm bebrebe yi, hɔn nyinaa bɔ kɔ Akyemfo kurow mu wɔakɔ akɔhwɛ aeroplane oo."

19.   REPORT ON HOSTELS AND BOARDING SCHOOLS IN CAPE COAST

A couple of very gracious ladies opened two hostels in the municipality. Young girls from about the age of ten and above were admitted and housed. Some children were locals while others came from neighbouring villages and other towns in the Gold Coast.
The young girls who attended primary schools, returned to the hostels after class and other required activities. At the hostels the girls were taught how to perform house chores, how to cook well and they also learned the intricacies of excellent dressmaking.

Mrs Dalrymple Hayfron affectionately called "Ewuraba Hostel" managed one of the hostels successfully. Young women were sent there to acquire graceful manners and learn to become good wives. The results of such training were quite satisfactory.

Mrs Faustina Daniels affectionately called, "Auntie Faustie" was the other charming lady who managed a hostel. Auntie Faustie was a very hardworking mother, who raised eight children of her own together with several nieces and nephews. She transformed the lives of several village girls into becoming fine, well-bred future wives when they attended at her hostel. Attending church service on Sunday was a regular feature which the girls enjoyed very much. They took to wearing fine dresses possibly to catch the eye of a young bachelor in the congregation at church. Cape Coast social life was said to be at its zenith at this time.

Typical conversation during this period between two friends:
"*Mansa, do hurry up, we'll be late for church again*", Baaba said impatiently from the doorway. It was a long walk to the church they were attending, from the hostels.
"*I am coming in a minute. Has Agnes gone ahead? I am sure she is in a hurry to show off her new dress in church*", Mansa remarked.
Baaba snapped back, arms akimbo. "*I must be in church before the choristers march majestically in, so do hurry up, please*".
"*I see! You have a crush on someone then?*" Mansa enquired, as she quickly grabbed her handbag.
"*Who? Me? Not at all!*" exclaimed Baaba.

20.   **THE RAINY SEASON**

Rainy season in the municipality brought much doom and gloom. Many roofs leaked and some mud houses collapsed. The wide gutters were no match for the volume of muddy water rushing through. The streets were littered with debris. As the drainage system in town was quite good, all water from gutters, rushed into the sea eventually.

Schools would be on vacation then: so many children in skimpy wear bathed in the rain outside their homes. When it stopped raining, boys would be seen using catapults to shoot small stones at birds for fun and games. They also played gutter to gutter football on the side streets.

Many infant diseases became rampant in over-crowded communities. Diseases such as measles, whooping cough and mumps would be on the increase as well as the usual malaria fever. The community health nurses worked very hard as infant mortality escalated. Children who suffered from mumps (an infectious disease), were treated carefully. A colourful array of red, black and white dots; using a thick red mud mixture made up of a ground charcoal mixture and white clay mixture would be placed on the painful swellings on the neck below the ears. If you had the courage to step out of the house you would be met with hoots of derision at the hideous sight of you covered in clay and shouts of "*Tsii oo Tsii*!" by young children would be heard whilst they ran away from you. This all made the ill person feel rather miserable, however the special spectacle had its uses. It was a way of informing the community about the fact that you had mumps and were infectious. Although mothers were quite protective of their children who suffered from mumps, they gave them roasted corn-on—the-cob in the belief that mastication would cause the pain and swelling to cease. Children succumbed to whatever they were asked to do, in order to relieve themselves of so much pain.

21.   **REPORT ON YULETIDE/THE CHRISTMAS SEASON**

Yuletide was enthusiastically celebrated during school vacation in December. Young boys built Christmas huts in their neighbourhoods using palm fronds. They would go together most evenings to their huts to drum and sing the latest hits for a few hours each day. The singing and drumming would carry on until Christmas day. In addition the boys would go singing from house to house for "treats or tricks" after which they returned into their huts to share and enjoy food items collected.

During the Yuletide season, several villagers would travel into town bringing farm produce which they would exchange for clothing they could wear on Christmas day in their villages. Many people showed much kindness, sharing the little they had with the underprivileged. Churches would be full to overflowing with worshippers.

Numerous visitors took gifts into hospitals to be given to the sick. Children enjoyed Christmas festivities most. They wore brand new clothing, socks and shoes and had a lot of goodies to eat.

Other Yuletide characteristics to note were the introduction of dances such as "High Life" dancing. "*Opul*", "*Osoode*", "*Adaha*" and "*Konkoma*" – dancing steps which appeared on the social scene were performed by youths and young adults at various gatherings.

Entertainment: Ballroom dancing was very popular and male adults attended in immaculate evening suits, bow ties and smart shoes. The young ladies also dressed to kill, for at such a function one might meet and dance with a possible suitor. They wore beautiful gowns with high-heeled shoes and had the latest hair fashions and gold or silver jewellery. They danced gracefully to the beautiful relaxing tunes of **Waltzs**, **Blues**, **Foxtrot**, **Quickstep** and **Tango**. Brass Bands accompanied such occasions and 'picnics', also known as street parades with masqueraders were very popular. Such spectacles were enjoyed by both young and old and several church groups and priests attended. In spotting a friend or relative among the dancers, one ran along and sprayed perfume on her, to encourage vigorous dancing and singing. It was such great fun!

At the end of Yuletide celebrations children would gather at "Bakatsir", near the Fosu Lagoon, to 'hoot' at Christmas and everyone played games and had fun while eating date palm fruit, which would be in season at that time.

Ocansey Cinema Hall and Cape Coast Town Hall Cinema, were the two places to see film shows from Hollywood. Amusing and musical films were delightful to watch and many people attended the shows. Some of the female stars adored by fans were Betty Grable, Ginger Rogers, Yvonne de Carlo, Veronica Lake, Dorothy Lamour and Deborah Kerr. The popular child star was Shirley Temple (who later became America's Ambassador to Ghana). The admired male actors were Clarke Gable, John Wayne, Cary Grant, Charlie Chaplin, Bing Crosby, Errol Flynn and Fred Astaire. Most of the songs sang by the stars, and other theme songs would be whistled on the streets of Cape Coast the following day of the big screening and fashions from the films were copied.

Typical conversation after a film show:
"*Clarke Gable is so handsome. He acts very well too. What do you think Susie?*"
"*I adore Cary Grant. Betty Grable dazzles one with her tap dancing, doesn't she?*" Susie asked, as she and Connie return home from Ocansey Cinema Hall.
"*I think Deborah Kerr is a very talented English actress*" remarked Connie. "*I enjoy musical films best. I can hum most of the tunes after the show. See you later.*"
"*Sure*". Susie replies, as the two young girls part company.

Plays were held at various venues throughout the country and "**Axim Trio**" was the most popular local concert party (or theatrical group). Fans packed the Cape Coast Town Hall long before the Trio came on stage. One of the male actors always impersonated a female character, wore women's clothing, spoke in a shrill voice and copied female mannerisms comically and the audience applauded loudly at the antics of the entertainers.

22.   COMMENTARY ON CAPE COAST SOCIETY's FINE MAIDENS

Many good-looking young girls lived in Cape Coast with their parents. There were, in particular some pretty sisters with delightful manners and poise living in various neighbourhoods and some notable ones were from the Williams, Daniels, Grant, Buckle and Brew-Butler families. Others were the Amissah, Nicholas, Elliot, Turner and Savage families to mention a few. Their brothers were equally handsome scholars. Many a father would direct a bachelor son to seek a wife from the home of such fine maidens who possessed 'no known malady' and usually the sons complied, with much success.

These fine maidens were sometimes referred to as "*Breeze!*" by secondary school students. At a social or church function, having spotted one lady, a young man would whisper the word, male heads would turn simultaneously to breathe in the "*Breeze*" as the girl was fragrantly passing by. It was all done in harmless good fun.

On such occasion, when a young maiden passed by, greeting a gathering of people on her way, the response to her could be "*Yaa, obi n'adze*" (if she was spoken for i.e. someone's property). The response to this comment would be "*Yaa, me dεε*" (meaning she belongs to me) and this could come from a would-be suitor with a hidden agenda to put his suit forward. All this occurred within a pleasant and enjoyable atmosphere which dominated the lifestyle of Cape Coast citizens.

23.   FUN-LOVING YOUNGSTERS

All societies have their hooligans and tricksters and Cape Coast was no exception. It had its fair share of young ruffians. They mainly hung around London Bridge and Turom in the town centre. Some of them were school drop-outs while others were witty illiterates who made general comments on the status quo as they lounged around and their remarks in Fantse on any affairs going on in the town would have you in stitches.

There also existed a group of young good-looking female streetwise drop outs and illiterate girls who enjoyed the company of the young ruffians and they insisted on following them around. The ruffians had the ability to coin one's name into the scathing lyrics of a Highlife song if one had the misfortune to have a confrontation with them so they were avoided by all and sundry.

Kɔbena Dadzie's "Always-Always" Palm-wine Spot at Siwudu Estates was well patronised by the male population. At weekends, under shady trees, the ruffians would gather to play games such as Ludo or Draughts, while quaffing palm wine contained in calabashes. Often late night parties were held at the Always-Always bar and this disturbed the peace of the Siwudu community as drunken shouts of "All in good fun" could be heard. The girls who enjoyed their company could be seen loitering around, laughing heartily at the jokes and antics of the drunk men.

Scenario at the Always-Always Bar:
A sudden shower of rain fell on the Always-Always bar. The girls scattered to shelter at a nearby porch of someone's estate house while everyone indoors was asleep. The men sat on the benches and got drenched. They eventually got up to leave as dawn approached.

"*Has it been raining, Jack?*" Abeeku asked, as he tottered unsteadily along the path.
Nana replies, "*Raining? You idiot, you are soaked. You got caught in the shower while singing in a falsetto voice and dancing your unique highlife steps to entertain the girls. And by the way, my name is not Jack. I am Nana Banyin Moses, remember?*"
Abeeku remarks, "*Oh, I see, so that is why I feel so wet. And where are we going, Mr Moses?*"
"*Home, of course, where you belong!*" retorts Nana Banyin.

24.   A DAY IN THE LIFE OF A PUPIL IN CAPE COAST

One woke up at dawn to go to the nearest standpipe for water, chewing "chewing-sponge" as one went along. Collecting water was a task given to young children in the household. As many containers as possible had to be filled with water to be used by people in the household. After the sweeping of rooms and other chores, one had a bath, wore one's school uniform, had breakfast and got ready to walk to school.

Breakfast would have been one of the following: (a) Tea, using condensed milk, and sugar bread with butter or cheese (b) Kenkey and fried fish or (c) Corndough porridge or rice water with bread.

One would then return home from school at lunchtime where any one of these dishes would be available: (a) Fufu[12] and soup, (b) Yam with garden-egg stew, (c) Rice with meat or Fish stew or (d) Spinach stew and boiled ripe plantain.

Pupils returned to school for the afternoon session which ended at about 4 o'clock. Supper in the evening was usually something light. It could be Jollof Rice or a special stew made with minuscule tilapia from the lagoon in Cape Coast to be eaten with kenkey were very satisfying. At night, girls slept on mats on the bedroom floor covering themselves with a sleeping cloth, and boys slept on similar mats on the floor in another bedroom. It was extremely warm weather as the Gold Coast is situated in the tropics.

Scenario: Friday afternoon conversation after school

"*Ebow and his sister Ama will join my sisters and me as we walk to Abura Village for firewood on Saturday. Other young people in our neighbourhood will also come along. What about it?*" Yoosi asked his friend Kuuku, after Friday afternoon classes were over.

"*I'm not sure if my mother will allow me to join you. She says it's tiring, and she does not want her only son to walk several miles from home to a farm for firewood*", replied Kuuku.

"*Be a sport Kuuku! Convince her with your charming manners and soft voice. We'll have fun gathering firewood; hiding a few plucked mangoes in the middle of the tied sticks and carrying the load on our heads. Come on!*" Yoosi cajoled.

"*What happens if the goddess "Samantan;" who has huge pendulous breasts suddenly appears to give chase for daring to enter her sacred grove?*" Kuuku enquired.

"*We shall outrun her through the overgrown paths. Her huge pendulous breasts will slow her down and we shall outwit her and become champions!*" exclaimed Yoosi.

---

[12]   Fufu is either pounded yam or plantain and shaped into a ball.

"It sounds exciting and adventurous fun for young, strong adolescents like us. I shall come along. What time do we start on Saturday morning?" asked Kuuku, whose face showed renewed determination.

Yoosi replied, *"We leave at dawn, at about four-thirty; walking, jogging, clapping, whistling hit tunes and singing patriotic songs. We shall return home by two-thirty in the afternoon. Cheerio for now Kuuku. Will be seeing you then?"*

"Sure, sure" Kuuku replied. Yoosi quickened his steps in order to get home early.

25.   GAMES PLAYED BY THE YOUTHS

Football: Exuberant young boys of Cape Coast played several games but football was fancied the most. Narrow playing fields were located in neighbourhoods where the youth gathered to play. They also watched their favourite football teams either <u>Mysterious Dwarfs</u> or <u>Venomous Vipers</u> playing at various matches and identified themselves with the best goal keepers and top goal scorers of a particular football match.

Wrestling was another game which boys enjoyed at weekends on the beach.

Top Spinning was a fascinating game too and this was how it was played:
A circular mound of sand or soil was slightly dented in the middle and covered with brown sheets of paper held down with stones around the mound. One's fingers were used to spin a top onto the brown sheet. Two or three boys would spin tops onto a mound depending on the width of its circumference. At times, two or more mounds could be functioning side by side with different groups of boys playing at the same time. Top spinning could also be played on a hard flat surface using a whip, by individuals.

Ampe: The girls had their favourite game which was called "Ampe". It was played by jumping and clapping their hands and by placing a foot forward, you were able to score a point. Hop-scotch, skipping, clapping of hands while standing in a circle and singing, were some of the other games enjoyed by girls.

"Asosɔw-Mba: A pebble game known as "Asosɔw-mba" was another game played by young girls. The idea was to form a group and play in turn. Even numbered pebbles were scattered on a flat surface. A single pebble was thrown up whilst two on the surface were picked without touching any others, before catching the descending pebble. It was a tricky but enjoyable game.

Kwãã- Kwãã/A Special Game of Hide and Seek: On a moon-lit night a special game of hide and seek known as "Kwãã- Kwãã" was played by both boys and girls. The following antiphony lyrics were sang.

Fantse version		Antiphony lyrics in English	
"Leader:	Kwãã- Kwãã	Leader:	Kwãã- Kwãã
Response by Children:	Yoo Yie	Children:	O-K-A-Y
Leader:	Alata mpuwa	Leader:	Banana from Lagos
Response by Children:	Ye nyim dzi	Children:	Edible
Leader:	Maane-maane ngo	Leader:	Mumbo-Jumbo
Response by Children:	Maane ngo	Children:	Mumbo
Leader:	Mereba oo denn	Leader:	I'm coming along
Response by Children:	Bra oo denn	Children:	Do come along
Leader:	Meba a mebɛkye ahen?	Leader:	How many can I catch?
		Children:	You'll catch ten.
Response by Children:	Ebɛkye du."		

By the time the Leader had finished singing the song, all the children would be hiding anywhere they could find, thus making it difficult for the Leader to catch hold of anyone. A child would then run to an agreed safe base shouting "*Akaayiee*!" which meant "I am safely home!" When all children got back home safely, the Leader had to start all over again. If a child was caught, he or she had to become the next leader. Children enjoyed the game very much as one had to be nimble in order to dodge and outwit the Leader and run quickly to the 'safe base'.

26.   COMMENTS ON HAND-MADE TOYS FASHIONED AND USED BY THE YOUTHS

Boys used Y-shaped twigs or branches for making catapults to shoot small stones at birds for fun and games. They also made simple bird cages using young bamboo sticks or other twigs and sold these cages to interested citizens.

The girls played with Fertility dolls which were carved out of wood, giving rise to intricate creativity. Clothing for such dolls were sewn by the girls. Dolls were also fashioned from sugar cane and were known as "**Ahwerba**".   A wrist to elbow length of sugar cane was flaked out and chewed at one end to represent hair. The flaked end was left in the sun to dry. It was then combed out and plaited with black thread or wool and could be woven or trimmed as one desired. Faces were painted on a side below the painted hair line. The sugar-cane doll was clothed and decorated with earrings and beads. Sometimes the little girls carried the doll on their backs tied with a cloth just as they had seen their mothers do with young babies and toddlers. Young girls met and displayed their "ahwerba-dolls" to each other and played with them for hours.

The young girls also made stuffed animals and rag dolls sewn from pieces of materials given to them by dressmakers and tailors. In those days, children were content to play with these home made toys.

27. ANANSESEM / SETTING THE SCENE FOR FOLKLORE STORIES ABOUT KWEKU ANANSE THE SPIDER

Kweku Ananse remained the shrewd trickster of Fantse Folkloric narratives. His wife's name was "ɔkɔdɔr", his son was "Kweku Tsen".

The story teller begun telling his story on a moon-lit night, to a crowd of children who had arrived. The story teller would call out, "*Kodzi wɔnngye ndzi o*!" (You are not supposed to believe stories told). The children would all reply "*Wɔgye sie (we will remember them)*", as they gathered round listening attentively.

When narratives were in progress songs would burst out intermittently from the gathering and some children would get up to dance, while others clapped and sang. The story teller continued telling the story while singing and dancing also continued until the end of the story. As the young children listened they learned how to tell stories in several different and interesting ways and even took turns in telling stories as the night wore on and subsequently everyone was entertained. The stories of Kweku Ananse the Spider, were full of tales about Ananse coming to a sticky end and pulling wool over people's eyes, but children learned standards for good or bad behaviour by listening to Ananse stories.

Other stories about "Sasabonsam" (a.k.a the devil) and his evil deeds were told and Satan never triumphed in such stories. Most of the stories were designed to have good morals for teaching children to acquire better foundations for growing from children to adolescents and into a meaningful adult life. One also learned of the good deeds or misdeeds of one's ancestors and their contribution to the people's welfare, society and the state in general.

28.   RELIGION IN CAPE COAST

About eighty percent of the population were Christians. The rest were either Muslims, also known as "Fantse Nkramo" or idol worshippers and animists known as "Abosomsɔrfo". The mainstream Christian churches were:

- Wesleyan Methodist
- Roman Catholic
- Anglican Church of England
- A.M.E. Zion a.k.a. African Methodist Episcopal Zion Church.

Other Christian Churches were:

- The Apostolic church nicknamed "Abɔnsamufo" which means "those who clapped at worship";

- The Faith Ministry nicknamed "Kyir bontoa" and the words literally mean "Refusal of any form of medication". Healing was dependent on faith only.

- The Nigritian Mission. Pastor Anaman, the founder, was nicknamed "Sɔfo Muoko" which translated, meant "the Pepper Pastor". He is best remembered for allegedly serving tea without milk and burnt toast at a Sunday school team party for children.

Christians believed and worshipped one God known in Fantse as:

Nyankopɔn:	Almighty Friend
Nyame:	You are full with him
Ewuradze:	Master
ɔdomankoma:	By his Grace
ɔbɔadze:	Creator

28.1   Sunday School Classes

Sunday School classes were held after church from 2.30pm to 4.30pm and they were very popular. School-going children and illiterate children attended wearing neat frocks for girls and shorts and shirts for boys. Adult illiterate women also attended in order to learn the Fantse letters of the alphabet, to write and also to read the Bible which was translated into Fantse. The letters **C,J,L,Q,V and X** are letters omitted in the Fantse alphabet. Educated Christian men and women joyfully made time to teach on Sunday afternoons without any form of payment. Illiterate women with typical Fantse names such as Esi Tekyiwa, Araba Adadzewa, Adwoa Efrima, Ekua Nyarkoa, Efua Apeawa, Aba Mensima, Esi Buabema, Ama Kwegyirba, Araba Seguwa, Ekua Tanoa, Ama Otuwa, Efua Sekyiwa soon found themselves writing their own names on slates using white chalk, to their delight.

They eventually were able to read simple story books such as the "Kofi na Ama" series and "Kweku a Oridzi Ne Dεw" books which were printed in the Fantse language.

A concert was held on the last Sunday School of the year when Bible verses, Psalms and Proverbs were impeccably recited in Fantse by 10 to 12 year old illiterate children. I remember *Corinthians 1: 13* being beautifully read by two illiterate elderly traders and applauded by the congregation, accordingly:

English version: "Though I speak with the tongues of men and of angels, but have not love, I have become a sounding brass or a clanging cymbal"

Fantse version: Sε medze nyimpa nye abɔfo tεkyerεma mekasa, na mennyi ɔdɔ a, mayε dε ayewa a ɔgyegye nye akasaa a ɔwosow..."

The congregation were entertained with short sketches based on Bible stories and the whole event was a great achievement for both teachers and less fortunate citizens of the municipality.

Other religions: Muslims worshipped a god known to them as "Allah" and their religion was known as Islam. They prayed in their Mosques and celebrated their feast days assiduously. "Abosomsɔrfo" or idol worshippers had numerous gods and goddesses which they worshipped and a few named ones were "Nana Paprata", "Nana Kumkensen" and "Nana Amissah". The different religious groups managed to live together harmoniously within the municipality.

29. SHORT REPORT ON THE ANIMISM CULT/FETISHISM – PRACTISED BY IDOL WORSHIPPERS& TRADITIONAL WORSHIPPERS

Fear of the unknown drove many people to visit fetish shrines in Cape Coast. They believed in "Mame Water" – an African mermaid animist cult. A few people kept bronze idols in the shape of "Mame Water" hidden in a bedroom which they used to invoke her appearance for desired wishes and to improve situations. Many believers went to the beach at midnight to invoke her presence to request for magical powers, wealth and good health.

"Samantan" was a goddess with pendulous huge breasts believed to be living in sacred groves in the forest. She was believed to kidnap children to the top of tall trees in her grove for several days feeding them on fruits only. Special rites had to be performed before the children were released unharmed but in a state of shock. It was alleged further that young girls who had had such experiences developed large breasts at puberty. Fetish priests and priestesses were custodians of such shrines of deities in the municipality and priestesses went about their normal duties naked from the waist up with either one calico cloth which was tied round their waist to end at the knee or wearing a raffia skirt. A necklace of cowries was worn criss-crossing the bare chest and back. People consulted at shrines through fetish priest or priestess requesting the destruction of an adversary, for loss of money, property or even as a result of a family feud.

A few fetish priests/priestesses were herbalists and after consultation with their gods they were able to obtain the right leaf or root from the forest. Roots, leaves, tree barks, vegetables and fruit juice were used in all sorts of healing procedures such as drinking, rubbing, inhaling and taking herbal baths and the fetish priests were rewarded in cash or in kind by villagers for their cures. A fattened white sheep with no blemish usually accompanied all thanksgiving items. Failure to present anything would bring the return of the sickness so patients usually complied.

An example of a cure: Ginger, tiny green peppers and a few shallots, were marinaded for a day or two in a pot of palmwine and this potion was supposed to cure coughs, colds and chest pains. Chewed charcoal was another remedy used to cure minor eye ailments. As a result of the high incidence of illiteracy, other herbalists learned the cure for both physical and mental diseases from their grandparents in the oral traditional manner. In order for a cure to begin, patients were required to present a live white chicken and six eggs to begin ceremonies. In those days the cure for mental illness of a patient was by the presentation of a white live sheep and a bundle of cloth to the shrine.

SCENARIO: The Sacred Grove Episode Of Prospect Hill

The wooded Prospect Hill straddled Kotokuraba and Ewim Roads in Cape Coast. Dwarfs lived in the woods, it was alleged. Delicious fruit trees formed part of the grove, however it was believed that one could get abducted by the dwarfs if one strayed into the orchard and special rites would have to be performed before the lost persons could be delivered at dawn usually suffering from shock and amnesia.

Many citizens avoided the shortcut to the path on the hill from Kotokuraba to Ewim Road to avoid being kidnapped. Personal names were never mentioned in conversation as people walked along the footpath and names of vegetables or fruits were mentioned instead.

One afternoon Araba and her three friends, Aba, Esi and Ama decided to skip art lessons at school and go by the bush path to pluck some unripe guava fruits on the guava tree nearer the path.
"Please call me "Muoko", (pepper)" Araba said to her friends as they began to climb to the hill top.

"*I shall be known as "Ntorɔba", (garden egg)*", whispered Aba.   "*What would you call yourself Ama?*" Aba asked her.

"*Atadwe," (tiger nut)*", giggled Ama "*What about you Esi?*" they all asked.

"*I think "Santom" (sweet potato) would do*".

Araba then, recited their new temporary names, pointing to each girl in turn.

"*Araba- Muoko*". "*Aba – Ntorɔba*". "*Ama- Atadwe*" and "*Esi-Santom*".

It was not difficult climbing up the hill and n no time at all they found themselves on the footpath where they decided to sit down on the grass and rest for a while.

"*I'm so thirsty!*" exclaimed Esi.

"*Here take these two toffees, Santom, they'll quench your thirst. I am glad I brought a packet along,*" mentioned Araba.

"*Thank you so much Muoko*". "*Can I have a couple please Muoko?*" asked Ama.   "*Oh yes, why not Atadwe?*" "*Now Ntorɔba, you can have some too.*"

After resting the girls got up and run along the path to the guava trees they could see. Araba volunteered to climb, and the others helped to push her up on to a branch. She plucked several unripe guava fruits but a few fell on the ground beneath the shady tree while others rolled along the path. The young girls quickly gathered them into their lap bags and even began eating one or two of the fruits. Araba (still up on the tree) shouted that she could see a wonderful orchard a few feet from where they were.

Suddenly without warning the sun set, and darkness and fog descended upon them.

"*Santom!*" "*Ntorɔba!*" "*Aradwe!*" *where are you?*" screamed Araba, suddenly feeling uneasy. She just managed to get down from the tree, when the girls heard the patter of tiny feet hurrying towards them.

They yelled to each other. "*Run Atadwe!*" "*Faster Muoko!*" "*Run Santom!*" "*Run Ntorɔba!*". The girls run as fast as their legs could carry them. All guava fruits collected were lost in flight as they scrambled through the undergrowth until finally they found themselves at Ewim Road in broad daylight, to their utter amazement.

They swore not to breathe a word of their adventure to anyone.

"*I guess we did enter the twilight zone*", sighed Araba.

"*Never again*", mumbled Aba, Ama and Esi.

They all headed home, a much wiser bunch of girls.

CHAPTER III
POST WAR YEARS: 1939–1945

POST WAR YEARS: 1939-1945

30.   PROFILES OF 4 DISTINGUISHED MEMBERS OF SOCIETY

Kofi Mensah Dadzie Esq.

Outstanding Educationists:
Mrs Mercy Kwarley Ffoulkes-Crabbe (neé Quartey-Papafio)
John Mends Samuel Pobee Esq.
Rev. Samuel Richard Stephen Nicholas M.A. DTh. M.B.E.

A.   **Kofi Mensah Dadzie Esq.**

Kofi Mensah Dadzie, was a prominent businessman in Cape Coast from the early 1940s. He set up a food supply store at "Bakano"[13] where he received fresh produce from farmers in the nearby villages. Kofi Mensah Dadzie was a transport owner who sent his lorries to buy foodstuffs from the villages, which he in turn supplied to Schools, Hospitals and Prisons. He also supplied transport to schools whenever students were going on excursions and trips outside the school compound.   Mr Mensah Dadzie thus had a monopoly regarding transport arrangements within the Cape Coast area.

Mr Mensah Dadzie had also acquired a large tract of land at "Aquarium", a suburb of Cape Coast, where he built his house, set up a poultry farm and a piggery. Products from these farms were *then* supplied to the institutions.

B.   **Mrs Mercy Kwarley Ffoulkes-Crabbe (neé Quartey-Papafio): Outstanding Educationist and Women's Organiser**

Mrs Mercy Kwarley Ffoulkes-Crabbe was the daughter of Dr Benjamin William Kwatekwei Quartey-Papafio M.D. (Edinburgh) O.B.E., the first medical doctor of the Gold Coast[14] and Madam Hannah Maria Ekua Duncan of Cape Coast and Elmina. Mrs Ffoulkes-Crabbe began her elementary education at Wesley School Cape Coast and Accra Grammar School (which was founded by her father and a few others). She obtained the College of Preceptors certificate as well as the Junior Cambridge certificate and became the first girl in West Africa to hold the certificate in her favourite subject – Latin.   Later on she spent 2 years at Saxenholme School, Birkdale Southport in Lancashire, United Kingdom, where she

---

13   A suburb of Cape Coast
14   The Gold Coast colony became independent from the British Empire on 6th March 1957

was taught the rudiments of teaching and then taught at a kindergarten before returning home in 1915 where she continued to teach.

Her ability to work soon came to the notice of the education authorities who made her Headmistress of <u>Cape Coast Government Girls School</u> (GGS), a position usually reserved for Europeans. As Headmistress of GGS for twenty-seven years, Mrs Ffoulkes-Crabbe was reputed for her dynamism, new ideas and strict discipline. She introduced several new innovations such as the wearing of school uniforms and initiated the first Parent Teacher Association (P.T.A.) in the Gold Coast and was the first to introduce Domestic Science as a subject into the school curriculum. As a result of this exercise, many of her past pupils became successful proprietresses of vocational institutions.

Under her care there was an intensive and extensive study carried out on the living conditions of girls attending GGS. Visits were made to homes and markets before lessons were planned and syllabuses drawn. A new playground for playing the game of hockey was installed at the school. Girl Guides was reorganised in the school and a Brownie Pack was introduced for younger girls. (see section on Girl Guides.)

Mrs Ffoulkes-Crabbe was a very religious woman. She inculcated the principles of Christianity and the importance of Christian living in all members of the school community. Her Friday morning scripture lessons at the school hall where the whole school assembled at 9.a.m. were unparalleled. As she was not fluent in Fantse, she would speak English which was translated by the teacher on duty. One Friday, her text was "The way of the wicked is an abomination to the Lord" (**Proverbs 15:9**). The staff member incorrectly translated it to mean God did not like wicked people. Mrs Ffoulkes-Crabbe calmly told her that was *not* what she said and went on to state in perfect Fantse **"Emumuyefo kwan ye Ewuradze ekyiwadze"**, to the utter surprise of the staff and girls. Ewuraba whispered to Sarah, sitting next to her, "Let's face it, the old lady has clearly shown us the right way to achieve success in life". Sarah agreed with her.

Teachers were kept on their toes to maintain high standards of teaching. Mrs Ffoulkes-Crabbe had such a tremendous impact on schoolchildren, teachers and parents and as a result many baby girls were named after her in many communities of the municipality. Her great concern for higher education of girls and women was highly respected. Mrs Ffoulkes-Crabbe inaugurated the following:
1.   The Young Ladies Association
2.   The Ladies Reading Circle
3.   Red Cross Society - (as a foundation member)

Mrs Ffoulkes-Crabbe was awarded the Member of the British Empire (M.B.E.) by King George VI in 1949. She received the award and insignia from Governor Charles Noble Arden Clarke.[15]

C.   John Mends Samuel Pobee Esq.

Mr John Mends Samuel Pobee was the son of John Mends Samuel Pobee (a.k.a. Kofi Kakraba) who was a Timber Merchant of Eguabado, Saltpond[16] and Mprukaimu[17], Cape Coast, and Mercy Dada Orleans of Ntoto, Cape Coast.

John Mends attended **Methodist & Government Boys' School (Cape Coast)** for his elementary education (or what we now know as primary school) and later attended SPG Secondary School (Cape Coast). He then went on to train as a Teacher at the **Government Teacher Training College** at Kinbu in Accra. In those days when travelling to and from Accra the only available transport was by sailing boats, since appropriate/direct roads had not been constructed. John Mends started his teaching career at the age of 16 years. He was so young and so short that he had to stand on a box to teach the rather grown-up pupils.

John Mends furthered his education later when he studied for and passed the Licentiate Certificate (both Junior and Senior levels) of the **College of Preceptors** and managed to obtain the highest mark for the Senior Preceptors examination for the whole of West Africa during his time and won the accolade, "The Pride of West Africa". Latin was his best subject and to make up the number of subjects required he surprisingly chose domestic science which he passed creditably. As a consequence of John Mends' achievement, the study of Domestic Science was introduced into the curriculum of Government Girls' School Final/Passing Out examinations.

John Mends' teaching career led him to teach at the Government Schools of Accra, Esiama, Oda (Nsuaem), Obo, Enchi and Cape Coast. He was best remembered as a Headmaster in the various institutions and also for the 'dreaded' Friday morning tests which were carried out throughout the school from classes in Standard 1 to classes in Standard 7. The tests were known as the Transfer Certificate tests. In addition, in order to help students, John Mends organised study sessions at his residence free of charge. The content of the educational programmes he established and the methodology of transfer of knowledge systems characterised him as a first-class Educationist.

---

[15]   Governor of the Gold Coast.
[16]   A town situated near Cape Coast. See map at rear
[17]   A suburb of Cape Coast

When John Mends retired from Cape Coast Government Boys School, he was appointed onto the staff of Adisadel College (a secondary school) at Cape Coast where he taught Latin, Geography, History, Algebra, Geometry and Arithmetic. He also taught English Grammar and Literature. John Mends was not only a distinguished and brilliant Educationist, but also a great Scholar. His expositions of Latin Classics were excellent.

Master Pobee, as he was commonly referred to, was a great *church goer* and Church Counsellor for many years. He was both a chorister and a lay reader in the Anglican church and retained the title 'Head Lay Reader' for years until he began to have problems with his eyesight. He enjoyed playing lawn tennis and thought early morning walks were good exercise. A strict disciplinarian, John Mends abhorred idleness, aimlessness and untruths! He believed in the idiom "*spare the rod and spoil the child*". He educated his children well and did not neglect his extended family either and was therefore the titular head of the Orleans family in Cape Coast for many years.

D. Reverend Canon Samuel Richard Stephen Nicholas M.A. D.Th. M.B.E.

Samuel Richard Stephen Nicholas (**"SRS"**) was born in 1899 and died in 1971 by which time he was the Reverend Canon Nicholas. It was a life of service to his fellow man.

While young Nicholas was at the SPG[18] Grammar School in Cape Coast his intelligence was discovered by the Rt. Rev. Mowbray Stephen O'Rourke, second Bishop of Accra. After a brief European tour with the bright fifteen-year-old, Bishop O'Rourke sent him to complete his secondary education at the C.M.S. Grammar School in Freetown, Sierra Leone, after which he entered the University College at Fourah Bay. Nicholas graduated from there with a Masters degree in Arts (Dunelm) and a Diploma in theology (D.Th.). He returned to the Gold Coast (as Ghana was formerly known as) and joined the teaching staff of his old school, the SPG Grammar School in Cape Coast.

Nicholas was in many ways the connecting link in the history of Adisadel College through its three developing stages – firstly as the SPG, then as St. Nicholas Grammar School to finally Adisadel College and Secondary School. Samuel Richard Stephen Nicholas served this Institution for nineteen years as the Classics Master, Second Master/Deputy and Headmaster. He was a superb classical scholar and his greatest gift was that of a teacher. Nicholas introduced Greek to the Grammar School when he was its Headmaster, thus placing the School on a pinnacle which inspired other secondary schools to emulate. He produced and directed Greek plays with professional competence. In addition to a fatherly interest in the progress of his pupils, he had a marvellous mastery of the technique and art of imparting knowledge to others. To boys and teachers alike Nicholas had an attractive personality and radiated energy, scholarship, discipline and his presence commanded respect. He made a great impact on the school and his far-sighted vision led him to initiate the negotiations for the hill on which Adisadel Secondary School still stands. From such a school and out of such hands, many a pupil emerged to carve out a fine career for himself and achieve distinction in later life.

After SRS left Adisadel College, he went on to Nigeria where he taught Classics at schools in Lagos. He later became the Headmaster of the Ijebu-Ode Grammar School for twelve years and went on to head St. Andews College in Oyo State, Nigeria. He was ordained a priest of the Anglican Church at Christ Church Cathedral in Lagos in 1944. He was awarded an M.B.E.[19] by **Queen Elizabeth II** for his services to Education, in Nigeria in 1957.

Reverend Nicholas returned to Cape Coast and taught his favourite subjects - English, Greek and Latin at various secondary schools for another 8 years during which he was engaged in the pastime of writing his own translation of the "*Antigone of Sophocles*" from the original Greek version. In a citation of the 75th Anniversary celebration of Adisadel College, it was stated "It is said that Education is the only interest worthy of the deep, controlling anxiety of a thoughtful man. Samuel Richard Stephen Nicholas made a happy and wise choice in devoting his life to education..".

He was a distinguished brilliant Headmaster and Scholar of Adisadel College Cape Coast.

---

[19] Member of the British Empire - an award given for outstanding achievement in your field of work.

31. INFORMATION REGARDING THE GIRL GUIDES ASSOCIATION – CAPE COAST

Mrs Mercy Ffoulkes-Crabbe re-introduced and reorganised the Girl Guides Association to Cape Coast Government Girls School (GGS) with the addition of a Brownie Pack for younger girls. She trained leaders and held camp meetings. Mrs Ffoulkes-Crabbe was the Captain, the Guide Commissioner and a member of the Executive Committee of the Girl Guides Association and was awarded the Certificate of Merit.

Camp meetings were an event everyone looked forward to. On one such organised camp meeting during the War Years the event lasted 3 days. It was held at Eyifua village, 5 miles north of Cape Coast. On this occasion the Guides who had passed their 'Tenderfoot Tests' were eligible to participate. Thirty members of the **2nd** Cape Coast Company of Government Girls School (GGS) arrived at the village on the first day in 2 trucks with their camping equipment and ingredients for cooking. Permission had been sought and granted for the use of a country lodge belonging to a prominent barrister-at-law. The lodge was situated on a large plain surrounded by mountains and was to be used as a temporary dormitory for the Girl Guides, instead of putting up tents. Facilities available to the guides were adequate. The Girl Guides were divided into patrols and Patrol Leaders were in charge of the girls, who were quickly settled in at the lodge on arrival.

Each patrol group had their tasks well prepared and carefully planned and the winners would receive a prize. The tasks were to:

a) use dry twigs and leaves together to light a fire with a single match;

b) whistle signals and successfully perform flag signals on the nearby mountain slopes;

c) follow Signs marked on barks of trees, or on the ground with arrows pointing to correct routes leading to the end of the search. This brought about so much mirth as the girl guides went round in circles trying, in vain, to read the tracks correctly.

d) compose the Union Jack flag of Great Britain and Ireland as we know it today. This was to be written down and coloured on plain sheets of paper. Crayons were provided. The 3 flags to be drawn correctly were:

(i) A red cross on a white background: being the Cross of St. George (England);

(ii) A white diagonal cross on a blue background: being the Cross of St. Andrew (Scotland)

(iii) A red diagonal cross on a white background: being the Cross of St. Patrick (Ireland).

e) exhibit the correct Full Salute and the Half Salute. Marks were awarded to Guides for the perfect salutes.

On this particular occasion, "Ewurabena's" Patrol members excelled and won many prizes. In the evening the girl guides sang 'Guiding songs' before bedtime followed with prayers and the girls loved every minute of it. The Commissioner would then visit the 'camp' on the last day where she would congratulate the girls for such good camping activities before they returned to their various homes with happy memories.

32. ADVENT OF KAYA-KAYA MEN/EDURO-EDURO MEN/MOSHIES DURING THE WAR YEARS

Kaya-Kaya Men: From the northern territories of the country came strong men who worked as head porters, to Cape Coast during the War Years. They also performed all kinds of jobs to earn money and became known as 'Kaya-Kaya' men. They usually carried items on their heads hence their name which was literally translated.

Eduro-Eduro Men: Eduro-Eduro men or herbalists a.k.a. medicine men arrived in town mostly from Mali and other north African countries. They carried sacks on their backs which contained herbs, roots, tree barks and other concoctions for use to cure ailments such as impotence, infertility, mental health, Parkinsons disease, malaria and other fevers. Childrens' illnesses such as measles, whooping cough and convulsions were alleged to be effectively cured by these men.

Moshies: Moshie men were originally from Burkina Faso (formerly Upper Volta) who migrated to Kumasi and eventually arrived in Cape Coast in search of jobs. They were a tall, hardworking, weather-beaten and virile people who were ready to enjoy the pleasant lifestyle that existed in the various communities they settled in. Soon Ekua Mosi, Araba Mosi, Aba Mosi and Kofi Mosi were children born to some petty traders in the neighbourhoods where the Moshies lived. One of the occupations they performed was to go from house to house with empty sacks collecting empty bottles and containers of various shapes and sizes. These would be washed clean and sold in markets and nearby clinics for use as receptacles to store palm oil, groundnut oil, shea butter, kerosene and various lotions and medicines.

"*Morn, Morn, Mame[20], any 'Bodambo-Bodambo*" (meaning any empty bottles available?)?" Sulaiman[21] would ask as he knocked on doors as he passed by or as he walked along the street. The presence of these tradesmen would encourage housewives to store any empty bottles and containers which they could then sell cheaply to the Moshie men. From time to time the Moshie men also worked as messengers. Never a dull moment for the macho men who came from the northern counties!

---

[20]   Short version of 'Madam' – a respectable form of address.
[21]   Generic name for any Moshie man.

33.   **SCENES OF APRIL FOOLS DAY**

Scenario One: The Long Long Walk

On the first day of the month of April, citizens of the municipality took the mickey out of the Kaya-Kaya men, Eduro-Eduro men and Moshies. A number of boulders concealed in a quantity of sawdust tied into a large sack would be carried by a head porter/Kaya-Kaya man. The heavy load was to be delivered to a businessman of a fake house number at Chapel Square from Aboom Road. Now, it was a long walk from one end of the town through busy Commercial street to the supposed destination. The head porter, having no idea of what he was carrying save that it was labelled "handle with care" in capital letters stuck to the outside of the sack. The porter would know the route but not specifically the house number. Muttering to himself the porter would say he would find the house. A few yards of walking along the road, beads of perspiration glistening on his brow, which he wipes off from time to time with his hand. It is very hard going. A few youngsters tagging along urge the porter to go on, each time telling him the house he was looking for was nearby, every time he asks! Paul and Eddie are aware it is an April Fools day joke but the head porter has never heard of it. Paul shouts to the head porter "*Mr Koomson's house is the third house on the right, when you turn left, not far at all*". Paul adds, "*He is a wealthy man and he'll pay you two pounds sterling for such a valuable load*". As the poor man struggles on, a number of young persons follow discreetly at a distance whispering "*April Fool! April Fool!*". The porter, exhausted now and perspiring profusely in his faded shirt and khaki shorts comes to a halt. An elderly man helps him to bring down the large sack and explains April Fools Day to him. Together they open the sack to find large stones and saw dust, to the utter surprise of the poor head porter. It is now Twelve Noon and April Fools Day is officially over. The porter had earned nothing and he was hungry, tired and angry! The elderly gentleman has pity on him and gives him a single coin to buy lunch and receives grateful thanks from the head porter who shakes his head as he leaves - a wiser man.

Scenario Two: April Fools Day : A Trip to the Dispensary

A Moshie collector of empty bottles is told to hurry to a private clinic where many villagers had gone to see the doctor. They needed bottles for their medicines from the pharmacy. The instructions were to wait until midday when more villagers would turn up. The Moshie collector is hopeful of big sales that day and hurries to the clinic with a large sack containing bottles. He finds only 3 patients and they have brought their own bottles for quinine - medicine for malaria fever. The villagers tell him to wait for the rest of the villagers to arrive. The Moshie man sits down and waits - but no one comes. It is now one o'clock in the afternoon. The pharmacist in charge of the Dispensary is closing shop to go home.

He smirks and says "*Don't you know today* is 'April Fools Day'*?* "*What be dat*" asks Abdul Moshie. "*First April is 'April Fools Day*". "*So, I be 'April Fool then?*", Abdul enquires. "*Maybe, maybe not*", the pharmacist replies, "*but I'm going home*". And on that note he left, leaving Abdul sitting on a bench outside the dispensary to his fate.

Scenario Three: April Fools Day: An Incomplete Errand

Most people in the municipality were slightly fearful of the "Eduro-Eduro" men (or herbalists) because they believed they possessed magical powers to cure ailments. One might even fall ill by executing any mischief involving them. They were therefore spared any pranks on April Fools Day and were left alone to peddle their herbs.

One fine day, Yokodwo[22] and his sister, Ama are sent by their Uncle Yokwamena to deliver a beautifully wrapped parcel to "Auntie Burenyi[23]" - a Mulatto lady living at Gyankober[24] Junction. Halfway down the road, they decide to unwrap the parcel out of curiousity. It contains down feathers of ducks that their uncle rears for a living. The naughty siblings burst out with laughter, quickly wrap up the parcel neatly again and saunter down the road. Suddenly they come face to face with two Eduro-Eduro men. The children decide to offer the parcel in exchange for magical cowrie shells (which they can play with). The men agree and one man accepts the parcel, while the other suddenly scares the children off by pulling out a live harmless snake and shaking it at them. The children take to their heels and never look back. The herbalists put the parcel in one sack and calmly carry on their way to have lunch at their usual eating place. After lunch, they open the parcel and are startled at what they find. They feel bewitched by the sight of the ducks feathers and in uproar, jump up and throw away both their bogus herbs (which they feel have been contaminated) and the feathers. They then rush to the Mosque for prayers to their god, Allah, to forgive them for their sins and protect them from any witchcraft that may harm them. The irony of it all! The Eduro-Eduro men later return home promising to be just and fair always.

Meanwhile YoKodwo and Ama return home to their parents and neither breathes a word about their prank. Meanwhile, their uncle, Yo-Kwamena, assumes all is well on that April Fools day and basks in the knowledge that Auntie Burenyi is thinking kindly of him and his 'lovely gift'!

22	Fantse version of the day name - Kodwo (boy child born on Monday)
23	Burenyi - a term meaning 'white man/woman' used to described light skinned or mulatto men and women.
24	Gyankɔber is a suburb of Cape Coast

34.   A SATURDAY TRIP TO KOTOKURABA MARKET

Scene I:

Background: Baba Awudu, Chief Butcher at Kotokuraba Market was very popular with the ladies who came to the market on Saturdays to buy choice cuts for the weekend's cooking.   He had a pretty daughter, Mariama, who helped her mother to sell 'Tuo' (mashed rice shaped into a ball) which was served with delicious palm-nut soup mixed with herbs – a favourite of the Muslims.   The butcher's stall was patronised by many workers who turned up at lunchtime on Saturdays at Mama Awudu's spacious stall where Mariama would serve with a big smile thus making all customers feel truly welcome.

Three students from the <u>Honest Boarding School for Boys</u> arrive at the stall for lunch on a Saturday to find a long queue of people waiting to be served.   Gerald, one of the braver (and dare I say, the better looking of the three) walks over and the following conversation ensues:

"*Hello Mariama, my friends and I are hungry, very hungry and we have to be back at school very soon, can you kindly serve us now, please?*" he pleaded.
Mariama replies "*Sure, why not, but how come you know my name?*"
Gerald slyly replies, "*Our friend, Mustapha, a day student, told us about you and your sweet smile so we've come to enjoy the food served 'with smiles' too.*"
Mariama smiled sweetly and says "*Oh, I see, follow me into the hall and I'll soon serve you*".
Gerald whispers, "*You are an angel, do just that and thanks a lot, 'M'! Can I call you that?*"
Mariama smiles and nods whereupon Gerald whistles for his two friends to come over.
"*How did you manage this?*" they ask, nervously avoiding the looks of the angry people in the queue.   Gerald enthused "*Charm, my brothers, charm pure and simple!*".

The boys finish eating and pay the bill waving Mariama goodbye as they return to school.
Gerald remarks as they walk along, "*I shall certainly be back to see "M" next week!*"
And the pals added, *"We shall certainly come along too, the food is very filling*".

35.   KOTOKURABA MARKET – THE VEGETABLE SELLER'S STALL

Scene II:

Background: Mame Sekyiwa was a favourite vegetable seller in the market. On Saturdays, her stall would be usually stacked with a dozen or more large baskets full of produce like garden-eggs, pepper, tomatoes, shallots, onions, string beans and lettuce. Many girls who were sent to buy vegetables were specifically instructed to purchase from her and you could not avoid buying from her as the large stall was opposite the main gate of the market. Mame Sekyiwa also knew their mothers and the girls also attended school with her daughters.

Typical conversation that ensues:

Mame Sekyiwa asks her assistant "*Besema, tell Auntie Adoma's daughter, Helena Flynn, I am waiting for her to come to my stall.*" Besema walks over and gives her the message whereupon Helena rushes over to the stall and buys up a lot of vegetables for the weekend. Mame Sekyiwa smiles indulgently and gives her the largest tomatoes, garden-eggs and pepper she spots. Helena says "*Thank you very much Auntie Mame Sekyiwa*" who grins and replies "*Say hello to your gracious mother for me and go straight home from the market, do you hear?*"

Helena did just that – she did not visit her best friend Irene that day on her way home as she knew perfectly well her mother would check up on her – the "old girl network" was thriving.

36.   EVENTS AT ACQUAH'S HOTEL

Acquah's Hotel[25] on Kotokuraba Road housed a contingent from the West African Frontier Force. The hotel was a three-storey imposing building that had no lifts. Two innocent looking rascals boldly enter the hotel and ask at the reception to see Commander Jallow who lives on the top floor. Apparently, Commander Jallow is their late mother's first cousin and having heard on the grapevine how kind he was the youngsters intended to take advantage of him. Upon meeting the Commander Joseph begins, "*We are orphans living with our grandmother who is seriously ill in hospital now.*" Tears dramatically roll down their cheeks as Joseph continues with his story of hunger and poverty– "*We need money to feed ourselves until Grandma is discharged from the hospital.*"

The Commander has pity on them and gives them ten shillings each. The boys thank him continuously and race down the stairs to the reception only to come face-to-face with Modou (a young man about town who knows the boys rather well).

Modou queries, "*Hey, you boys, what are you doing here?*"

---

[25]   Sadly Acquah's Hotel is no longer standing.

They reply, "*We are just passing by and...*".

"*Well*", Modou harshly replies, "*You two better hurry up and go home now, NOW!*" He is aware that they were up to no good, but cannot quite put a finger on the problem.
The boys rush out and turning the corner, burst out laughing, "*We have earned one pound sterling today, just climbing stairs and shedding a few tears. On, on we go to London Bridge!*", they exclaim.

It is lunch time now and the boys are really hungry and they therefore head towards "Gyakye's Chop Bar[26]" located at London Bridge and where many rascals and drop-outs hang out. It is nearly full to capacity as they enter but they find two empty seats at the rear where they sit down and order rice, chicken stew and glasses of lemonade with their ill-gotten gains. Halfway through their meal Modou turns up and heads straight to the corner where they sit. As he approaches Joseph notices and comments:
"*Oh no!*". "*Here we meet again*" Modou remarks, "*feeding fat on delicious food while I starve eh? Tell me, where did you two get the money from?*"
Joseph replies "*Uncle Commander Jallow gave it to us, truly he did!*"
"*Well*", Modou says, "*I could do with some Fufu and Palm Nut soup[27] and are you ordering now?*" Modou settles himself down on their bench.
The boys exchange glances with each other and Joseph decides it is safer all round to go along with the request.
Joseph assures Modou by replying, "*Uncle Modou, Sir, it would be a pleasure to buy you lunch.*" The boys decide to go home after their hearty meal and pledge never to go near Acquah's Hotel ever again as the stress involved was just not worth it.

Meanwhile, Modou was quite happy with the free lunch he had "acquired" as life had been a little difficult over the past few days and money had been hard to come by. He suspects also that the boys might be telling untruths as "young con artists" do, as to how they had obtained the monies for their food but as he, Modou, had benefited from their escapade he would not enquire further.

The chop bar was emptying out since the lunchtime session was nearly over and Modou decides to go home and hit the hay. Tomorrow was another day.

---

[26]   "Chop Bar" is a term used to describe a road side café where lunch and dinner is served to working-class people.
[27]   Fufu and Palm Nut soup is a traditional Ghanaian dish.

37. INTRODUCING EGYA QUANSAH'S DAUGHTER VICTORIA & HER ILLEGAL TRIP TO THE CINEMA

The film "*Sentimental Journey*" a popular movie with an exciting soundtrack, was showing at the nearby cinema. Victoria asked her father if she could go to see this film as Maureen O'Hara, the star of the film was a favourite of hers and she was determined to go and see her. However Victoria's dad, the old spoilsport refused so a plan was hatched. Francis, Victoria's elder brother asked Musa his friend for assistance. Memuna, Musa's sister, would supply Victoria with a simple Muslim outfit and *Mayafi* head veil. Francis would wear one of Musa's Muslim outfits and sport a dark coloured fez. They needed this disguise because the only route to the cinema was via the front of the house onto the main street.

Paa Quansah, the father of Francis and Victoria, sat out on his front porch chatting and receiving greetings from passers-by that evening. He was surprisingly fluent in the Hausa[28] language and took the opportunity to speak it whenever he could. As part of the plan Hassan, Musa young uncle, had been roped in to leisurely pass by and engage the old man in serious conversation about the coming municipal council elections, a topic dear to Paa Quansah's heart. Right on cue during the conversation two Muslims wearing dark coloured fezzes would quickly walk past calling out in Hausa "*Memuna, Fatoumatta, hurry up please, we are running late*". Victoria (now renamed Fatoumatta) and Memuna, Musa's sister, skip out from the back door, and run along past the old man, deep in political conversation. He scarcely notices them. They join the two muslims walking along the road. As soon as they are out of sight of the house they whisk off the Muslim outfits revealing their normal clothes and place the outfits into bags the girls are carrying. All four people break into a sprint to arrive at the Town Hall in time for the movie, buy tickets and settle in to enjoy the film. The plan worked!

On their return home they find the old man *still* chatting with more candidates on his front porch. He is in his element because he has a huge audience now listening to his views. Victoria and Francis are let in through the back door by the housemaid and they go straight to their bedrooms. No sooner had Victoria tucked herself in with her sleeping cloth than up the stairs came Paa Quansah to look in briefly, only to find her 'fast asleep' in bed.

"*Such thrilling adventures should not be repeated though, for a while*," Victoria whispers to her brother the next day. Everyone is happy – Victoria and Francis watched their film, the housemaid who attended to Victoria's chores for the evening is given a few pence for her trouble and the old man had his 'fan club' on the porch!

---

[28] Hausa is a language spoken by people from northern Ghana who are also follows of Islam.

CHAPTER IV
COLONIAL PRE-INDEPENDENCE ERA AND SOCIAL AND CULTURAL ASPECTS

CHAPTER IV
COLONIAL PRE-INDEPENDENCE ERA & SOCIAL AND CULTURAL ASPECTS
(and other activities after the War Years)

38.   FIRST YULETIDE SEASON AFTER WORLD WAR II (circa December 1945)

The first Yuletide season after the end of World War II was a very exciting one. Apart from the usual charitable atmosphere and Christmas fever that people enjoyed very much, acrobats from Liberia poured into the municipality, staged hair-raising feats to the utter amazement and disbelief of the people watching the displays. 6 year old and 8 year old children were carried shoulder high by stalwart young men. The children were bare-chested and the boys wore shorts and raffia[29] amulets round their necks and the girls wore raffia skirts over their panties. As part of the acrobatic displays the children were thrown high into the air and then caught at almost ground level. Daring stunts with sharp knives (used to cut sugar cane), were seemingly used to slash the bellies of the children yet not a drop of blood was spilled. The show was held in an open field and the crowd who watched would hold their breath and whisper "Jesus" as these amazing acts occurred. An equally amazing feat was walking the tight-rope performed by 8 year old girls who fearlessly carried long poles to help themselves to balance. Stalwart men positioned themselves at suitable distances beneath the tight-rope for a quick rescue should an accident occur. The most thrilling part of the entertainment was when a very young girl walked the tight-rope blindfolded! A lot of money was collected daily for as long as the show continued and many inhabitants marvelled at the ease with which the acrobats performed.

As the girls walked home after watching the show Mensima enquired of her friend Tanoa,
 "What did you think of the belly-slashing feat?"
"I think it's a first-class performance by the young acrobats and they must have had lots of practice to achieve such a high standard." Tanoa replied.
"Would you agree to the usage of a sharp knife slashing your stomach?, Mensima enquired.
"Certainly not! Not even on my little finger let alone anywhere else", retorted Mensima. Giggling and nudging each other the girls parted company at Bakano roundabout on their way to their various homes.

---

[29]   Raffia - is made from woven grass and used to make skirts and body ornaments.

39.   THE ADVENT OF THE NEW BREED OF SOCIAL GIRLS

The festive season brought with it a new breed of "Social Girls". Some of them had completed elementary school (secondary school in today's terms) while others were drop-outs.

Auntie Rosa, Overseer to the Social Girls was a well-to-do businesswoman whose business was wholesale trading in onions. The onions were imported from Lagos in large bags via Auntie Rosa's elder sister who was married to a Nigerian business man. The Social Girls collected the bags of onions for retail during the week at various stores. As a result of the successful retail business activities the social girls became particularly well known. During weekends they became busy with social activities, especially on Sundays, usually after a thanksgiving service, which they attended as a group.

Fatima Drameh, a.k.a. Fati, was the leader of the group and she was slender, elegant and tall. The robust looking social girls caused quite a stir in the municipality as they began to get noticed. Auntie Rosa was always impeccably groomed as were the girls and she taught them good manners and etiquette and as saleswomen they were taught how to serve with a charming smile. Auntie Rosa specialised in Food, Fashion and Flower and the social girls excelled in these areas.

Often after a thanksgiving service in church, special guests and mourners would be asked to follow the widow to the house where finger food would be served. The job performed by the unique Cape Coast social girls and their Overseer Auntie Rosa was carried out for a small fee. They would meet the guests with smiles, usher them to comfortable seats and food would be served accordingly using good crockery. The girls would serve drinks followed by Jollof[30] rice and tossed salad and all this was executed with great style.

Fashion: As a uniform, the girls wore the slit skirt and "kaba" cover shoulder which was firmly introduced onto the Cape Coast fashion scene. As the social girls were hired out to serve food and drink at numerous high society functions they turned up in stylish long skirts which were slit along the leg and which had matching tops known as the "kaba" and performed their duties admirably.
One old lady was overheard asking the widow at the function, "*How on earth do these girls manage to walk nicely in the slit skirts and high-heeled shoes?*". The widow replied, "*I understand they attend an hour's practice three evenings a week at Auntie Rosa's hall. Music is played as the girls walk past and practice turning around several times until they become perfect under the watchful eye of Auntie Rosa.*" Auntie Tantri moaned "*What is this world coming to?!*' Uncle Billy, who had been eavesdropping all along tells his prim and proper sisters, "*Tantri, your youthful days are over and done with. Remember dancing*

---

30   Traditional Ghanaian rice dish served at parties – similar to Spanish paella.

the 'Charleston' in the 20's? Now it's the 'Jitterbug' and 'One Way' highlife[31] dancing which is now in vogue!'

40.   BEEN TO'S - RETURNED HOME

The return of the "Been-To's"(a term used to refer to those who had studied abroad and returned home) brought much joy and happiness to their proud parents, siblings and relatives during the war years (1939-1945). Young qualified lawyers, doctors, engineers, nursing sisters and many others were enthusiastically welcomed back home. Some of the Been-to's had acquired good diction of the English language and mannerisms of British people. It was noted that the Fantse spoken by these ladies and gentlemen had an Oxford accent. One such "Been-to" lady was the first to ride a bicycle down the streets of Cape Coast. On the first attempt, many children and young rascals gave her chase as she rode by, clapping and screaming at her. It was a unique spectacle to behold! The embarrassed lady got off her bicycle and pushed it along the road instead, for a while before resuming riding until the children got used to seeing her astride the bicycle.

Another lady who had returned home from her studies, went out to town one day in stockings and had gloves – an affectation she had adopted from being abroad. On meeting someone she knew she would shake hands with the person "*Aborekyirfo kyia kyia wo*", meaning "Greetings from abroad". This became her nickname for good. Everywhere she went from then on, she was greeted "Hello Ewurefua "aborekyiraba", the phrase meaning "Hello lady from abroad".

An example of the type of conversation would be:
"*Hello Aborekyiraba, I must say, that is a most becoming dress, my dear, it suits you so well*". Agnes would remark upon meeting her friend at Jerusalem Street.
"*This is just a summer frock I bought at a "Barkers" sale just before I sailed home. Wait until you see the one from "Derry and Toms, it is a beaut!*" Ewurefua would sigh pleasurably.
Agnes would then ask *"Where did you buy your pretty pair of shoes?"*
"*Saxone,*"Ewurefua would answer, totally oblivious to the fact that her friend had no idea of these shops not having travelled abroad. Ewurefua would continue, *"I have other fine pairs I bought from "Dolcis" and "Lilley and Skinner". These are top shoe shops in London's Oxford Street, you know!*", Ewurefua then explains.
Agnes then exclaims, *"Well, I hope to travel to London next year to pursue advance studies in midwifery and go shopping along the famous Oxford Street too!"*
"*You will, my dear, you will and I am sure you will study hard and return home an accomplished "Been-To"*, Ewurefua pleasantly assures her friend.
Agnes thanks her friend and wishes her a nice weekend.

---

[31]   'Highlife' describes elegant up to date Ghanaian style traditional dance performed in cities.

Scholarships were awarded to many more deserving persons to study various disciplines in the United Kingdom. They sailed away on board ships such as M.V. Apapa and M.V. Aureol. Since the voyage took eleven days to arrive in England, on board flirtations were not uncommon.

Events at The Turnabout Ballroom Dancing Club: Meanwhile back in Cape Coast the "Turnabout Ballroom Dancing Club" was refurbished which engendered a lot of excitement in the town. The club brought many young men and women together, including those who had returned home from abroad and enabled people to both learn and teach the intricate steps of the Waltz, Quick-Step, Blues, Foxtrot and Tango which were the latest dances of that era. The dancing club was well patronised and many young women of good breeding from respectable homes flirted with these 'men from abroad' at the Turnabout Ballroom Dancing Club.

"*Did you see that "Been-to" in church last Sunday?*", Connie shyly asked her friend Betty after choir practice on Saturday.
"*Who, the one with the crew-cut and sporting the trendy tweed jacket?*" Betty enquired.
"*Never mind, even though he is not that handsome, he is a lawyer from a respectable family. I shall make a beeline for him*". Connie giggled, "*Goodbye, Betty, see you in church on Sunday then.*"
Betty replies "*In your Sunday-best I suppose? Goodbye Connie, sweet dreams and good luck!*".

The war raging in Europe did not deter people from enjoying themselves. The young adults attended Variety Entertainments, Concert Parties and Cantatas which were staged at the Town Hall to help raise funds for the war effort.

Some of the "Been-Tos" contributed immensely to the success of such shows by joining the artistes in achieving brilliant performances and plays. The "Teenage Syndrome" of rebellious young persons doing their own thing was unknown at that time. Adolescents aged between thirteen and nineteen were known as "ABERANTSEϵ" for males and "AKATAASIA" for females and were addressed as such.

The incidence of Sexually Transmitted Diseases ("STDs") was minimal. Youthful promiscuity in Cape Coast society was frowned upon among the youth and young adults. It is in stark contrast to the promiscuity resulting in the pandemic explosion of AIDS and HIV which exists today among the world's youth. Energies of the youth and exuberant young adults was channelled into productive entertainment shows. It was quite astonishing to see the quality variety shows of song and dance performed by members of clubs such as the Top Drama Society. Numerous cantatas of musical works imbued with apt words were performed usually with themes based upon religious subjects. These themes were beautifully choreographed and portrayed by nimble-footed graceful dancers.

41.   PERFORMANCE BY TOP DRAMA SOCIETY

At one outstanding performance by the Top Drama Society at the Town Hall, the musicians raised the roof with several standing ovations. Some of the romantic songs that made the youth of "Abɔɔdzen Kurow Mu" tick, had these lyrics:

(a)   "If it rains, who cares?
For when 'am looking in your eyes
Am looking at the skies of blue...

(b)   For a while we must part,
But remember me Sweetheart
'Till the lights of London shine again...

(c)   What lovely weather? Hello!
Lovely, lovely weather. Hello!
How my heart is yearning, Hello!
To be alone with you. Hello!

And many many more ......!

"*Pharoah is King*" was the title of an unforgettable cantata performed at the Cape Coast Town Hall. It had carefully selected female dancers in elaborate costumes on stage with their exciting opening number which begun:

"HAIL, OH HAIL, OH HAIL!
Thou monarch of Egypt's land.
Hail! Thou monarch of Egypt's beauteous land.
HAIL! ....HAIL!..... HAIL!
Thou monarch of Egypt's land."

The choreographed entry of the youthful dancers was breathtaking. This was followed by the entry of King Pharoah and his entourage who all had superb costumes.

The next memorable scene was "The Prodigal Son" act. Uncle Ato Kwamena sang in fine baritone voice the lyrics below:

"I will arise and go to my father
and I say unto him: Father! Father! I have sinneth! I have sinneth
I have sinned against heaven and before thee.
And am no more worthy to be called they son.
I will arise! I will arise!
And go to my father - My F-a-t-h-e-r!"

The burst of applause after this rendition was deafening.

Next on stage came the nimble female dancers to the banqueting suite, for the feast of the prodigal son's homecoming. They sang and danced, carrying huge beautiful vases on one shoulder whilst weaving among the banqueting tables.

They sang:

> "Haste, the gorgeous banquet lay!
> Haste, the gorgeous banquet lay!"

The performance was splendidly performed and could very easily have won an award in modern times.

Someone in the audience shouted "*Long live "Abɔɔdzen Kurow Mu*". "Hip hip hurray was the general response. And that was the evening that was! Cape Coast citizens loved those shows which were pleasant and very enjoyable where they were able to relax.

Form of Address: Society was well ordered and respect for all adults was in place indicated where male adults were addressed and regarded as "Uncles" and female adults as "Aunties".

"*Me nua basia*", meaning 'my sister' was used as a form of address for young female adults. "*Me nua banyin*", meaning 'my brother' was used as a form of address for young male adults.

Young girls referred to male acquaintances as 'cousins', hence the term "CAPE COAST COUSIN" therefore "Cousin Yoofi" could well be just a nodding acquaintance but nothing more and cousin was just used in this instance as a form of respect.

Proper care and provision was made for the aged, senior citizens and the infirm which was organised by the extended family members system and therefore begging on the streets by senior citizens did not exist at that time. "Mame" was also a term used to address older women whose names one was not aware of.

42.   THE PLIGHT OF EX-SERVICE MEN

After the War, thousands of young men who had been conscripted to fight for the British in World War II (1939-1945) returned home, expecting when demobilised, to be provided for with adequate pension for their hard toils overseas. This did not happen.

Some ex-service men were maimed while others did not return at all. They had died while in service. While the ex-servicemen were fighting overseas, an amount of cash, known as the "Allotment", was sent home from overseas to wives, siblings, concubines, parents and relatives. The men demanded on their return, accountability of monies sent and some family members were able to explain away how the cash was spent. Guilty spouses and concubines who could not give an account, ran away to live in surrounding villages until the ex-Servicemen's tempers had calmed down. What could one do when an ex-serviceman who felt cheated and aggrieved approached in a rush, brandishing an axe towards his relatives because his money had been squandered by them. People would run helter skelter onto the streets in an attempt to escape harm. This was not a very good period in Cape Coast. Sanity would later be restored..... but much later.

Many stories of extreme bravery at the front line in far away Burma, were narrated to anyone willing to listen. There were many more stories of soldiers seeing 'Mame Water' or mermaids as they are known in the western world, in the Indian Ocean after rounding the Cape of Good Hope in South Africa who gave soldiers and sailors the "V" for victory sign as the mermaids swam in the sea. People listened to the weird stories which they took with a pinch of salt. *"Hmmm...! Really?...so?"* murmured the young listeners as the storytellers embellished their fantastic stories.

When shy young men were seen dating young ladies by strolling down the road while chatting, young lads would follow at a safe distance behind mischievously yelling

"War news, he's telling you, young lady. Don't listen to him."

Then roaring with laughter they ran past, leaving the lady in doubt as to the sincerity of the young man's intentions.

As the ex-servicemen gradually begun to settle into Cape Coast society, some of them set up micro business from the experiences they had gained while soldering abroad. Garages were soon opened to train the youths especially the drop-outs who loitered aimless during the day, in the town centres. The young boys enjoyed the welding and other car repair work which was being taught.

The ex-servicemen were also full of songs especially geared for route marches. Most of the songs had outrageous mirthful lyrics which were catchy and which the youth picked up readily. They sung, whistled and danced to these tunes all over town. As a result, youthful dance bands sprang up under the disciplined eyes of the ex-servicemen. The band boys wore fanciful costumes in order to attract people to attend the various venues where they played. Wealthy merchants and older music-loving men with cash to spare sponsored these youth bands. Musical instruments such as the double bass, saxophone for jazz music, brass band instruments such as the trombone, trumpet and percussion instruments became very popular. The bands became very popular and were hired out for parties, wedding receptions and other gatherings at a very reasonable fee.

As the music business boomed, there were some new arrivals. They were natives from Freetown, Sierra Leone and were so named by the inhabitants of Cape Coast as '*Papa Sa Lo*' and '*Mama Sa Lo*'. The Sierra Leoneans brought with them their own culture and food, introducing the Fantse people to their own brand of spinach stew called '*Palaver Sauce*' which was eaten with soft cassava[32] fufu. Palaver Sauce became quite popular with the

---

32   Cassava is a root vegetable. Gari grains are a by-product of cassava.

ex-servicemen who enjoyed being re-introduced to this dish which they remembered while being stationed in Freetown before going overseas. Students who studied at Fourah Bay College in Freetown and had returned home to Cape Coast also enjoyed the delights of Palaver Sauce.

43. PROSPERITY ARRIVES AT CAPE COAST

The population of Cape Coast soon doubled with the homecoming of both ex-servicemen and "Been-Tos". Many of these men asked for the hand of many a maiden in the town and bouncing babies were soon everywhere among the fisher folk and farmers. Midwives were kept busy rendering superb childcare services. Breastfeeding was the norm and the babies were well taken care of. At the Government health centre near Government Girls' School (GGS) babies who came in for weighing were well scrubbed, powdered with hair combed. They were dressed in clean simple chemises for girls and tiny shorts and vests for baby boys. Children belonging to ex-servicemen met their fathers for the first time and the fathers made everyone aware of how proud they were of their infants and promised to send them to school. Many Primary Schools were established in Cape Coast to facilitate education for female children among the lower income group at that time.

Trendy shops copied from those seen in the Far East were set up by demobilised ex-servicemen. Young girls and boys were employed as salespersons in these shops. One outstanding shop was known as the "Kofi Atta Rangoon Emporium" which was situated at Aboom Wells Road, where a large variety of goods was sold. Most of the goods came from the Far East where Kofi Atta had been stationed and had returned unscathed, to the admiration of his fellow soldiers. Goods from the Far East came to 'Uncle Kofi's "R.E." as citizens of Cape Coast called his shop. Any item one required could be found at the "R.E." and if he did not have it then the item could not be found anywhere else in town. Uncle Kofi's shop sold antiques, lace chair backs, shower curtains, screw drivers, crochet books, muslim outfits and "*Mayafi*" veils for muslim women. He also sold fezzes, knives, embroidered tablecloths, fanciful slippers - Kofi Atta's R.E. had them all! It was a shoppers paradise.

As profits increased, Kofi Atta opened a **"Chittagong Coffee Club"** for ex-servicemen only. The soldiers flocked to the club throughout the week where they were served by youngsters who offered them the special brewed coffee the soldiers had been used to in the Far East. Amusing anecdotes were told amongst themselves while sandwiches, rock buns and pies were sold at the club. Delicious cuisine was provided by Efua Atta, Kofi Atta's twin sister.

Law and order was upheld in Cape Coast with the help of ex-Constable Nii Ato Addy who was a fine policeman. He had endeared himself to the citizens of Cape Coast because he was kind, friendly and affable. He knew the important people in town and rascals always stood to attention and saluted whenever he passed them as he walked his beat. Many young boys called the Constable "Uncle Nii Police". On retirement, Ex-Constable Addy was invited to join the Chittagong Coffee Club ("CCC") of Aboom Wells Road. He would tell amusing anecdotes about his years as a policeman to the merriment of the ex-servicemen. Uncle Kofi Atta and Aunt Efua Atta's names became synonymous with hardwork and prosperity and good clean living.

44. EXPANSION OF EDUCATION IN CAPE COAST AFTER 1945

The people of Cape Coast enjoyed discussing education, education, education! It was their basic occupation. The establishment of many more primary schools was therefore in order, especially by the Catholic Mission which had efficient and trained female and male teachers. Children of farmers, fisher folk and other low income groups were enrolled and the education of girls was encouraged. The gender competition had truly begun.

45. STUDENT LIFE IN CAPE COAST/THE FORMING OF THE STUDENTS UNION

There was in influx of students into Cape Coast. As a way of obtaining admission into the sought after male-only secondary schools in Cape Coast, young adults from other areas of the country filled entry requirement forms with incorrect ages, hence the term 'mature students'. During the long vacation, many students stayed in town either living with friends and relatives where they feverishly studied in order to catch up with the studies at the beginning of the new academic year. A newly-formed "Students Union" held its first meeting at Richmond Hall near the Methodist Book Depot complex and many male and female students attended in their numbers to elect officers.

The phraseology used by Kuuku Essuman in his acceptance speech as the First President of the Students Union was hailed as a classic by all present. In addition, the appointment of a female student as Vice President was a quantum leap for Womens Equality.

At one of these meetings, it transpired there that Steve Smith, a fifth form student had written a lovely Sonnet to someone he admired, a certain Miss Sophia Mensah, a brilliant student. The last line of his sonnet was, "*To be or not to be, dear Pal*"? (Apologies to Shakespeare's Hamlet soliloquy). As a result of this poem, Steve Smith earned the nickname "*To Be*" thereafter.

The Students Union meetings were a great success. Picnics were organised at the beach behind Cape Coast Castle which activity attracted many more students of both sexes. On those occasions spontaneous limericks were recited by <u>Wesley Girls High School</u> students to the applause of all present. Delicious doughnuts, fruits, scones, sandwiches and other goodies were provided by the girls and shared while the boys presented the gathering with fruit drinks. Beachwear was strictly regulated – skirt and blouse for girls and boys wore shorts and vests or if they chose, were bare-chested. Serious swimming was not allowed for safety reasons, so students had to make do with walking barefoot along the shore line. Ball games were modestly carried out and at the end of the day everyone walked back home.

Holy child Secondary School for girls was to be another well known Catholic secondary school to be established in Cape Coast soon after the war in 1946. A bevy of pretty young girls arrived across from the southern part of the country and they had travelled from as far away as Keta in the Volta Region and Axim in the Western Region, the Ashanti and Eastern Region to attend Holy Child Secondary School. They were mostly from Catholic families and other Christian denominations and they joined the local girls from Cape Coast itself. Parents transferred their daughters from other schools to Holy Child because they were aware of the excellent tutelage under the Catholic nuns and efficient members of staff who run the school. The formidably intelligent girls became a force to reckon with in the fields of education, sports and debates. Competition was fierce among the secondary schools for the "Brains of Cape coast" contests between Mfantsipim Secondary School (which was a male-only institution) and Wesley Girls High School and a team was pulled together from both schools to form a Methodist orientated team. Adisadel College (a male-only secondary school) and St. Monica Secondary School got together to create a good Anglican orientated team. A third team known as "The Holy Children" was derived from students of St. Augustine's College for boys and Holy Child Secondary School for girls – an arrangement organised with the Papal blessing from Rome, apparently. Successful debates were conducted amongst the similar religious groups and the public were invited to attend where issues such as morality and conflict were discussed in a logical and forthright manner.

The University College of the Gold Coast, now The University of Ghana, Legon was established in the late forties. The first female graduate, Mrs Elizabeth Frances Sey (neé Biney) was born and raised in Cape Coast. Dr J.E.K. Aggrey, Achimota Secondary School's founding member once stated "If you educate a man, you educate an individual. If you educate a woman, you educate a family".

46. **AN EXCURSION BY STUDENTS TO ABURA VILLAGE** (A village a few miles From Cape Coast Town)

Scenario I:
The excursion was organised by the Students Union led by John Assam, leader of the Planning Committee. Students arranged to meet at Aquarium Avenue at 6.00 a.m. complete with water bottles borrowed from ex-servicemen. The girls brought along with them sandwiches, tea, Jollof rice, fried fish, kenkey[33] and gravy in their thermos flasks for the trip. After several miles walking along the dirt track while singing old colonial marching songs the group arrived two hours later at Abura village, where Egya Anaman

---

33   Kenkey is staple food derived from fermented corn and rolled into a ball wrapped with dried plantain leaf.

Esq. had his sprawling maize farm.

After a quick breakfast the students were taken to the farm to help harvest all the maize.

"Scorpion"! Scorpion!" screamed Rachel as she jumped away from a twig on the ground. *"Where is it, where is it?"* shrieked Emma to her friend. They then both noticed a tiny brown baby scorpion in the undergrowth. Emma stamped on it to kill it with her canvas shoe. Everyone became a little more cautious after that incident – it was better to be safe than sorry. Lunchtime could not come soon enough.

Egya Anaman decided to treat everyone to boiled corn-on-the cob in appreciation of their hard work. The students were also allowed to pluck several mangoes from the orchard and the girls were able to avail themselves of pepper and garden eggs to take back to Cape Coast. Work stopped just before sunset and the leader, John Assam, thanked Egya Anaman for his gifts and Egya Anaman responded that their work was much appreciated. The students boisterously left the farm, already planning which farm they were choosing to visit next. This arrangement suited everyone concerned both from the farmer's point of view and the students.

47.   SCENE OF A WAKE-KEEPING HELD AFTER WORLD WAR II

Usually on a Friday evening, the body is laid out on a special brass bed. Prayers are said by priests while people file past for a last viewing. Mourners are give cola nuts and peeled sliced ginger which they had to chew in order to keep awake. Priests and male choristers were served with hot coffee, hard boiled sweets to aid the singing of funeral hymns that carry on until midnight.

At the wake-keeping of a wealthy "Bagyirbanyi" businesswoman, the deceased was adorned with gold and silver jewellery and rings on her fingers. She had a classically beautiful face that had little need of adornment. Her many friends and associates turned up in their numbers to wail her death. After 2 hours of wailing mourners were requested to go to the breakfast room for coffee. On their return they found the body had been dressed in expensive lace. Another change of velvet clothing replaced the lace several hours later and finally her last outfit, a beautifully sewn shroud was placed on her. A white beaded necklace replaced the gold and silver jewellery and her friends murmured "She is at perfect peace with herself". Indeed a fitting farewell!

At that time there existed a small "Band" made up of some unemployed ex-servicemen who had teamed up with some youths who played the accordion and they usually were invited to attend wake-keepings. After the choristers leave they were usually replaced by the ex-servicemen. These men could sing without hymn books, especially all the verses of a popular funeral hymn "Abide with me" and for their efforts they were given the local gin[34]. Sometimes this is their undoing as they begin to sing outrageous songs instead of mournful ones.

Scenario at a Wake:

On one such occasion, the band having known the deceased person was a teacher, began to sing school songs the teacher might have taught. The band proceeded to put up a specific show - classification unknown! They produced a blackboard, duster and chalk and performed a sketch of the teacher at work, while singing at the same time! The ex-serviceman would write numerous figures on the board to be added up using fantastic methods of calculation to arrive at zero - which was the correct answer. This act they believed to be a fitting farewell to the illustrious teacher! Mourners gazed in amazement at the events before their eyes but could do nothing about it as the group were in their element.

---

[34]   The local gin is known as Akpeteshie (made from the palm tree) and is very potent.

On a separate occasion where the deceased was a fine lady of ballroom dancing fame, a pair of the youths displayed Tango steps accompanied by music from an accordion ending with the solemn words "*Lady, moonlight becomes you!*" to the horror of all who observed their antics. The events of the evening continued until 4.00 a.m. when mourners left to prepare for the funeral service at church the following morning while the extremely drunk and rowdy bunch of ex-servicemen and youths went home to sleep off their hangover.

48.   KWAME NKRUMAH'S MEMORABLE STORMING VISIT TO CAPE COAST

At the end of the decade of the '40s, the Gold Coast Colony seemed to be going through a phase of awareness and the political climate was changing. Enthusiasm for politics was engendered in the youth and young adults by a certain charismatic personality known as Kwame Nkrumah.

Kwame Nkrumah arrived home to the Gold Coast in 1947, and took up the post of Secretary-General to a political party known as the United Gold Coast Convention (UGCC). Shortly afterwards, however, in June 1949, Nkrumah broke away from the UGCC and launched his own political party which he called the Convention Peoples Party (CPP). On one occasion, rumours were rife of a pending visit to Cape Coast for a political rally at Victoria Park. Long before Nkrumah's open-top car was perceived at the outskirts of the town, Victoria Park was teaming with people anxious to catch a glimpse of the man they had all heard about – Nkrumah. Many others who could not get into the Park where the rally was to be held, lined Commercial Street through to "Amrado Yard" Government Gardens (streets that led to the Park). There was an air of scarcely controlled excitement in Cape Coast!

"Kwame Nkrumah! Show Boy!" someone shouted. *"Osagyefo[35], come and rescue us from the yoke of imperialism!"*, others cried out as the elegant car came into view. There was the singing of catchy party songs and street dancing of all types resembling a carnival as the crowd followed his retinue along the main street of Cape Coast. Nkrumah waved his trademark white handkerchief to the crowd of eager faces, acknowledging their cheers with broad smiles. He knew he had been well and truly accepted by the citizens of Cape Coast. The appellations of 'Show Boy' and 'Osagyefo' remained his alone, forever. The political rally was a huge success. As if on cue, Auntie Rosa's Social Girls elegantly mounted the platform wearing stunning outfits in the CPP colours – red hats with the symbol of the red cockerel.

The crowd roared and clapped with delight, whipping themselves into a frenzy as the Social Girls chanted the slogan *"CPP" means "Si no Pi Preko*!". The crowd took the slogan up "Forward ever, Backward never!" The crowd poured into the streets singing all sorts of slogans and dancing long after the politicians had left.

Older politicians on the sidelines gaped in awe at the scene unfolding before their very eyes. The next day CPP party activists enlisted thousands of youthful members and they issued party cards at various neighbourhood centres and collected dues.

---

[35]   Osagyefo means someone who is coming to deliver us from war or servitude.

Fati Drameh, Leader of the Social girls announced the formation of the Women's Wing of the Convention Peoples Party at Aperase constituency and as a result many prosperous women joined.

"*We shall soon be recognised as First lady Mayoress and her Deputy and the first course begins in a fortnight.*", Paulina informed her friend Joyce, as they went on their way to check progress at a registration centre.

Joyce replies, "*That will be a great day since 'Uncle Kwame' waved his handkerchief directly at me and I responded with mine.*"

"*Hello, Hello Joycey, the man waved at everyone and not you in particular!*", Paulina reminds her friend.

Joyce retorts *"Let us bet on it and watch me, Auntie Mayoress to be!* "*Si no Pi Preko, CPP for you.*" As they reach the venue Joyce gives her friend a knowing smile.

Kwame Nkrumah spent a few more days in Cape Coast consulting with senior members of his party behind closed doors, no doubt to plan their strategy. They also met briefly at the grounds of St. Augustine's College and then continued to Sekondi (another town in the Central Region). As the entourage departed many students lined the streets to bid him farewell waving their white handkerchiefs. It was quite a scene to behold. The CPP team Nkrumah left behind were a formidable group of intelligent, efficient trained professionals some of whom had studied abroad and returned home ("Been-Tos") and therefore they understood the brand of Socialism that was being put forward.

A well attended bazaar called the "*Si No Pi Preko Bazaar*" took place at Government Gardens, "*Ambrado Yard*", to raise funds for the coffers of the CPP party. Large posters depicting the red cockerel and 'Osagyefo' brightened up the streets of Cape Coast. Red rosettes were sold at the entrance as the gate fee and people registered their names and pinned the rosettes on to show their solidarity to the party. The Social Girls arrived wearing old army fatigues and were in charge of sales in the stalls. Cape Coast cuisine was at its best and available to the public at reasonable prices. The public attended because the bazaar was also a family-day-out and there were a lot of competitions and fun to be had by all.

During the week, at the CPP party headquarters in Beaulah Lane, if anyone indicated they had a party card, had paid their dues and wore their red rosette a senior member of the party would offer a scholarship form to fill in order to pursue any discipline of study that was desired in countries such as Russia and Romania, Bulgaria and other countries of Eastern Europe. Many young men and women registered, applied and obtained scholarships thus the race for the foundation of a new breed of "Been-Tos" had begun after the War Years.

SO BE IT - THIS WAS THE NEW MODERN WORLD.

GLOSSARY

Term	Explanation
"Abɔbɔe"	A popular cooked large bean dish made with palm oil or cooking oil and served with ripe fried plantain.
Abongo Boys"	Irresponsible young men who have left town to avoid having to maintain pregnant girlfriends.
"Abosomsɔrfo"	Idol worshippers
Aggrey beads	Beads of a superior quality originally to be found in streams – used on ceremonial occasions.
"Ahwerba"	A sugar-cane doll fashioned out of chewed sugar cane for young girls to play with.
Bagyirbanyi	The term was applied to a well-to-do stylish woman engaged in brisk trading business.
"Cape Coast Cousin"	Term used by young girls/adolescents to refer to friends and acquaintances in Cape Coast.
Chewing sponge	Chewing sponge is the dried bark of a tree which has medicinal qualities and is used as a precursor to toothpaste.
Coalpot	A small crude metal cooking stove which is stoked with charcoal in the lower compartment.
Compound House	A large walled one-storey building of several individual units made up of a bedroom, kitchen and bathroom with a shared courtyard usually occupied by family members/tenants.
C, J, L, Q, V and X	Letters which are not present in the Fantse alphabet.
"*Etsew*"	"Cooked corn dough
Fufu	Pounded yam, cassava, green plantain and shaped into a smooth ball usually to be eaten with soup.
Highlife	Popular music of the day which incorporates traditional rhythms of Ghanaian music.
Jollof Rice	Rice cooked into a highly spiced tomato stew to produce a pleasant orange colour and served with meat & vegetables.
"Highlife" Music	Traditional music with an upbeat modern rhythm which is singularly native to Ghana
Kaba	Top half of the traditional cloth worn by ladies.
Kenkey	Fermented corn dough shaped in a ball and wrapped in plantain leaf and cooked – usually served with fish, shrimps, stews and other sauces.
Kente cloth	Colourful rich hand-woven traditional cloth which is worn on ceremonial occasions.

Konkosifo	Term used to identify group of mainly elderly illiterate women who engaged in petty trading of all kinds of goods from their homes.
Konkosinyi	Singular of term (Konkosifo) describing an elderly female trader.
"Mame Alata"	A colloquial name used to refer to Nigerians in Cape Coast.
"kɔtɔ"	A dish which contained boiled and mashed yam smoothly mixed with palm oil with a few slices of hard boiled egg decorated round the dish – used to celebrate occasions such as weddings, first menstruation and puberty rites.
Outdooring Ceremony	A ceremony performed on the 8th day to celebrate the birth of a child. The child is normally named on this day.
Palanquin	Covered seat/couch for a chief usually carried on the shoulders of 4 strong men accompanied by a large traditional umbrella
Palm Wine/Akpeteshie	Potent local gin derived from the palm tree.
Pampamu Store	Store (containing goods for sale) in the form of a tray or box carried on the head of the salesman
Raffia	A local type of yarn resembling grass
Vernacular	ɔ – sound pronounced as in <u>o</u>range/<u>o</u>ctopus/<u>o</u>strich ɛ – sound pronounce as in <u>e</u>xample/<u>e</u>arth/<u>e</u>cho
Wax print	A bundle of 6 yards of fairly expensive cotton print (made in Holland) which was highly regarded and used by women to sew their kaba and cloth.

LIST OF ILLUSTRATIONS

Photograph Number	Description
Photograph No. 1	Mr John Mends Samuel Pobee – a distinguished brilliant Educationist and Scholar, Cape Coast
Photograph No. 2	Dr (Mrs) Mary Stoove Grant (neé Duncan). She was a Fantse female medical doctor, who rose to become a Member of the Council of State.
Photograph No. 3	Reverend Nicholas, Priest of the Anglican Church.
Photograph No. 4	Mr Samuel Richard Stephen Nicholas – a distinguished brilliant educationist and Scholar, Cape Coast
Photograph No. 5	Mrs Mercy Kwarley Ffoulkes-Crabbe (neé Quartey-Papafio) – An outstanding educationist and Womens' Organiser. She is also the Guide Commissioner of the Girl Guides Association.
Photograph No. 6	Mrs Elizabeth Frances Sey (neé Biney). The first Fantse female graduate of University college of the Gold Coast.
Photograph No. 7	The Author, Mrs Augustina Korsah, in her youth.
Photograph No. 8	Kofi Bentsi-Enchill Esq. He was the first appointed black African managerial agent of United African Company – U.A.C. Limited
Photograph No. 9	Mr Gilbert Acquah (popularly known as Uncle Ato Kwamina, the author's uncle – an example of an ex-Serviceman who returned home to the Gold Coast from the Far East, safe and sound.
Photograph No. 10	Kofi Mensah Dadzie Esq., a prominent businessman in Cape Coast, with daughter Doris, the apple of his eye.
Photograph No. 11	The Author and her children
Photograph No. 12	Two "Beentos"[36] – those who studied abroad and returned home: Kofi Mensah Dadzie Esq. and Dr Kweku Abakah Boison (Dental Surgeon).
Photograph No. 13	Mr Kofi Annan, United Nations Secretary General being interviewed by Kwaku Sakyi Addo, a renowned Ghanaian journalist.
Photograph No. 14	Cape Coast Town Hall
Photograph No.15	"Oguaa Akɔtɔ" Monument, Cape Coast
Photograph No. 16	"ADAASO" – Dream come true. Residence of Kofi Bentsi Enchill in Cape Coast.
Photograph No. 17	University of Cape Coast entrance gate
Photograph No. 18	Centre for National Culture, Cape Coast

---

[36]   A term which indicates that the person referred to has travelled abroad.

Photograph Number	Description
Photograph No. 19	Central Regional Hospital, Cape Coast[37]
Photograph No. 20	Victoria Park, Cape Coast.
Photograph No. 21	Victoria Park, Cape Coast.
Photograph No. 22	Bust of Queen Victoria at Victoria Park, Cape Coast.
Photograph No. 23	Cape Coast Castle – side entrance
Photograph No. 24	Girl Guide – Tenderfoot Test Guide No.1 Girl Guide – Tenderfoot Test Guide No. 4
Photograph No. 25	Map of Ghana (formerly known as the British Colony of The Gold Coast
Photograph No. 26	Young men pulling or dragging net to the shore – Cape Coast.
Photograph No. 27	Fosu Lagoon Cape Coast (facing the Atlantic Ocean).
Photograph No. 28	Fosu Lagoon Cape Coast (abode of *"Ebia" Tilapia,* a famous Cape Coast fish delicacy).
Photograph No. 29	State Transport[38] Bus Stop – Cape Coast
Photograph No. 30	Anaafo Market, Cape Coast
Photograph No. 31	Downtown Cape Coast.
Photograph No. 32	Birds eye view of Kotokuraba Market, Cape Coast
Photograph No. 33	Entrance to Kotokuraba Market
Photograph No. 34	Inside Kotokuraba Market, Cape Coast
Photograph No. 35	Signpost of Kotokuraba Market, Cape Coast
Photograph No. 36	LONDON BRIDGE, Cape Coast (x2)
Photograph No. 37	Tantri Road
Photograph No. 38	Coronation Street
Photograph No. 39	Downtown Cape Coast

---

[37] This is the main and largest Government hospital in the Central Region area

[38] State Transport – Government owned/sponsored inter-city buses.

1. Mr John Mends Samuel Pobee

2. Dr (Mrs) Mary Stoove Grant (neé Duncan)

3. Reverend Nicholas.

4. Mr Samuel Richard Stephen Nicholas

5. Mrs Mercy Kwarley Ffoulkes-Crabbe

6. Mrs Elizabeth Frances Sey (neé Biney)

7. Mrs Augustina Korsah (neé Buckle) in her youth.

8. Kofi Bentsi-Enchill Esq.

9. Mr Gilbert Acquah (ex-Serviceman)

Kofi Mensah Dadzie Esq. and daughter Doris

The Author and her children

Two "Beentos" - Kofi Mensah Dadzie Esq. & Dr Kweku Abakah Boison

Mr Kofi Annan interviewed by Kwaku Sakyi Addo

Cape Coast Town Hall

Crab Monument, Cape Coast

"ADAASO" – Dream come true. Residence of Kofi Bentsi Enchill.

University of Cape Coast entrance gate

Centre for National Culture, Cape Coast

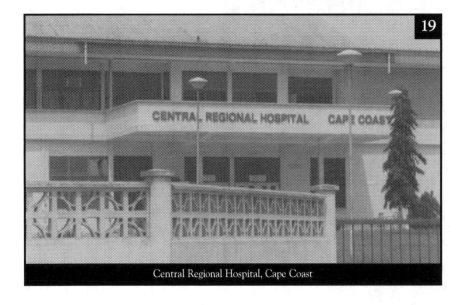
Central Regional Hospital, Cape Coast

Victoria Park, Cape Coast.

Victoria Park, Cape Coast.

Bust of Queen Victoria at Victoria Park.

Cape Coast Castle – side entrance

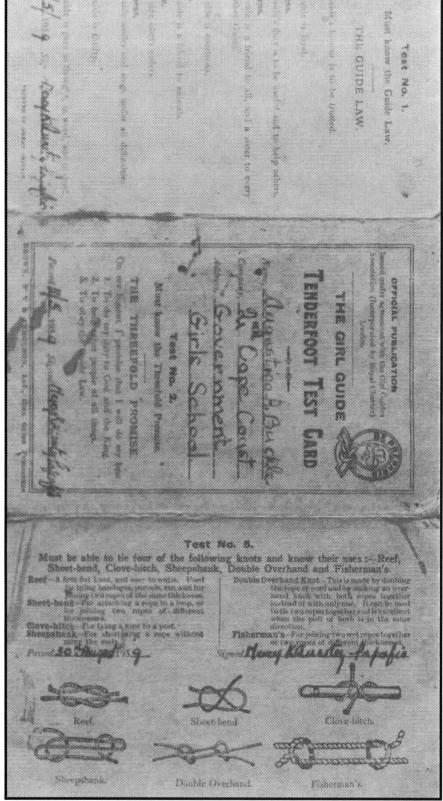

Test No. 4.

Must understand the composition of the Union Jack and the right way to fly it.

Flag No. 1 is the Cross of St. George (England).
Flag No. 2 is the Cross of St. Andrew (Scotland) added to No. 1 in 1606.
Flag No. 3 is the Cross of St. Patrick (Ireland) added to No. 4 in 1801.
Flag No. 4 is the first Union Jack (adopted in 1606).
Flag No. 5 is the Union Jack (adopted in 1801).

The right way to fly the Union Jack is with the broader white stripes at top next the Staff. If flown upside down it is a Signal of Distress. If at half-mast it is a sign of death or mourning.

The Union Jack is the National Flag of the United Kingdom and the British Empire and is made up of the old National Flags of England, Scotland and Ireland. In 1606, King James VI. of Scotland, who was also James I. of England, added to the flag of Scotland (which was a Blue Flag with the White Diagonal Cross of St. Andrew) a Red Plus Cross with a White Border to represent the Flag of England (which was a White Flag with the Red Cross of St. George). Thus the Scottish and English Flags were blended to form the first British Union Flag. In 1801 a Red Diagonal Cross to represent the Flag of Ireland (which was a White Flag with the Red Diagonal Cross of St. Patrick) was added to the Union Flag making the Union Jack of Great Britain and Ireland as we know it to-day.

Passed *24th August* 1939. Signed *Mary K. Austin Lupton*

Test No. 5.

Must know the Signs and Salute.

THE SALUTE OR GREETING SIGN.

Full Salute, with right hand to hat. Three fingers upright, thumb and little finger bent and touching; elbow in.

Half Salute, the same, with the hand raised only as high as the shoulder, used when out of uniform, or without a hat.

The three fingers held up reminds the Guide of her threefold promise.

SIGNS.

Road to be followed.	Turn to the right.	Letter hidden at number of paces indicated, in direction of arrow.	Path not to be followed.	I have gone home.	No. 2 Wren Patrol, 17th Glasgow

WHISTLE SIGNALS.

A long blast :—"Halt," "Silence," "Alert," "Lookout for next signal," or "Cease."

A short blast :—"Attention."

A succession of long blasts :—"Go out," "Go farther away," or "Advance," "Extend," or "Scatter."

A succession of short blasts :—"Rally," "Close in," "Come together," "Fall in."

A succession of short and long blasts alternately :—"Alarm," "Lookout," "Be Ready."

Three short blasts followed by a long blast :—"Leaders come here."

HAND OR FLAG SIGNALS.

Hand or flag held high and waved quickly from side to side at full extent of arm, means—"Close in," "Rally," "Come here."
Hand or flag pointing in any direction, means—"Go in that direction."
Clenched hand or flag jumped rapidly up and down several times, means—"Run."
Hand or flag held straight up over head, means—"Stop," "Halt."

Passed *17/8/* 1939 Signed *Mary K. Austin Lupton*

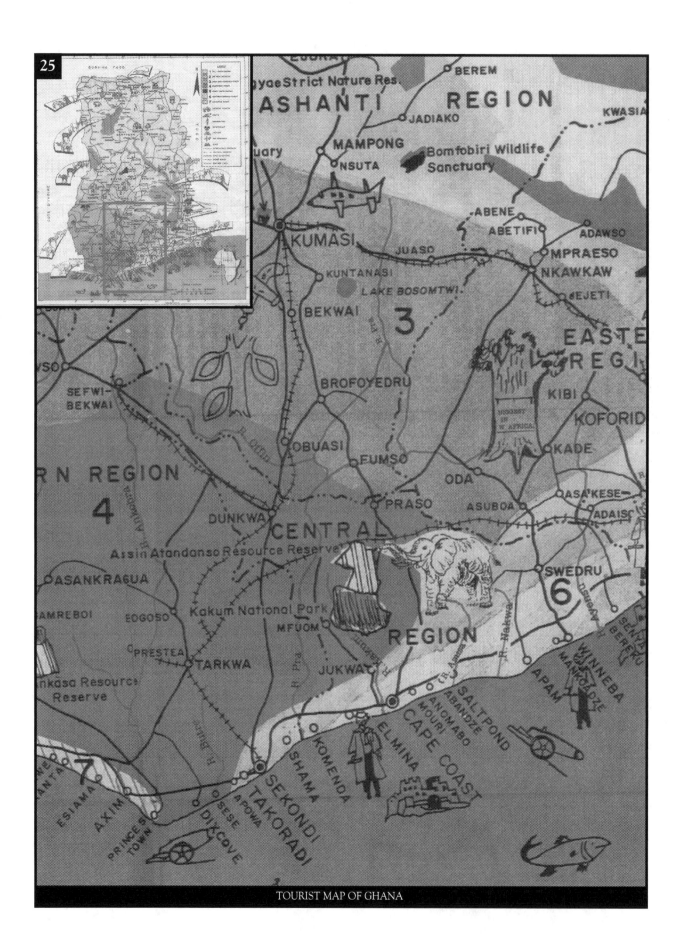

26 Young men pulling or dragging net to the shore – Cape Coast.

27 Fosu Lagoon Cape Coast.

28 Lagoon-abode of "Ebia" Tilapia fish

29 State Transport Bus Stop – Cape Coast

Anaafo Market, Cape Coast

Downtown Cape Coast

Birds eye view of KOTOKURABA MARKET

Entrance to Kotokuraba Market

Inside Kotokuraba Market, Cape Coast

Inside Kotokuraba Market, Cape Coast

36

LONDON BRIDGE, Cape Coast

LONDON BRIDGE, Cape Coast

37

TANTRI ROAD, Cape Coast

38

CORONATION STREET, Cape Coast

39

DOWN TOWN, Cape Coast